the
poetry
of
Shelley

the poetry of Shelley

This edition published in 2018 by Arcturus Publishing Limited
26/27 Bickels Yard, 151–153 Bermondsey Street,
London SE1 3HA

Copyright © Arcturus Holdings Limited

All rights reserved. No part of this publication may be reproduced,
stored in a retrieval system, or transmitted, in any form or by any
means, electronic, mechanical, photocopying, recording or otherwise,
without prior written permission in accordance with the provisions of
the Copyright Act 1956 (as amended). Any person or persons who do
any unauthorised act in relation to this publication may be liable to
criminal prosecution and civil claims for damages.

AD006345UK

Printed in the UK

Contents

Introduction

One of the best known of the English Romantic poets, Percy Bysshe Shelley (1792–1822) never achieved the recognition that some of his peers did during his own lifetime. It was only after his death that he was hailed as a visionary poet.

Shelley was born into a privileged life as the eldest son of Sir Timothy Shelley, a landowner in Sussex in the south of England, and attended Eton College and Oxford University, where he purportedly went to just one lecture but spent up to 16 hours a day reading. However, he was sent down from Oxford in 1811 after the publication of a pamphlet called 'The Necessity of Atheism' which enraged the university's authorities.

Some months later, in August 1811, Shelley eloped with a 16-year-old friend of his sisters, Harriet Westbrook. It proved to be a bad match, and he later fell in love with Mary Wollstonecraft Godwin, the daughter of the writer William Godwin by his first wife, the writer Mary Wollstonecraft. In 1814, Harriet, by then pregnant with their second child, returned to her parents' home, and Shelley and his new love, who was only 16 herself, ran off to Switzerland.

Shelley and Mary Godwin eventually married two years later, but only after Shelley's estranged wife was found drowned in the Serpentine in London's Hyde Park. The couple enjoyed travelling in Europe. They had three children (although the birth of a fourth child was registered in Naples, it is uncertain as to whom the little girl's mother was): the two eldest, William and Clara, died in 1819 while the family was living in Italy, but their third child, a son named Percy Florence Shelley who was born after the deaths of his brother and sister, survived them.

The family settled down to life in Italy, moving around between cities such as Florence, Pisa and Rome. Shelley continued to correspond with many of his contemporaries, including Leigh Hunt and Lord Byron with whom he intended to set up a journal to be called the *Liberal*, and to follow political events around Europe that inspired many of his poems and other works. Whatever plans Shelley may have had, though, came to an abrupt end on 8 July 1822 when he and two companions drowned during a storm while returning to Lerici from Livorno. Shelley's body was recovered and cremated at Viareggio, after which his ashes were interred in the Protestant Cemetery in Rome.

During his lifetime, Shelley tackled various forms of writing, from poetry to plays and even gothic novels, as well as writing essays on politics, religion, free love and vegetarianisim. This anthology includes many of his best-known poems, such as the sonnet 'Ozymandius', the odes 'To a Skylark' and 'Ode to the West Wind' and 'The Mask of Anarchy', plus a number of his longer, visionary poems like 'Alastor, or The Spirit of Solitude' (considered to be the first of his major poems), 'The Daemon of the World' (the reworked 'Queen Mab') and 'Adonais'.

'Mont Blanc' highlights the influence of other writers such as Wordsworth, Coleridge and Byron, but also reflects Shelley's love of the natural world; while poems such as 'To Jane: The Invitation', 'To Mary Shelley' and 'To Sophia (Miss Stacey)' record Shelley's relationships, romantic and platonic, with some of the women in his life. Jane was Jane Williams, a naval officer's wife of whom Shelley became very fond, and Sophia Stacey was the former ward of his uncle and aunt.

Although informed by his political conscience and a strong philosophical idealism that gave him a deep desire for social justice, Shelley's work stands out for the quality of its imaginative vision, use of symbolism and an intense appreciation of beauty.

The Devil's Walk

Once, early in the morning, Beelzebub arose,
With care his sweet person adorning,
He put on his Sunday clothes.

He drew on a boot to hide his hoof,
He drew on a glove to hide his claw,
His horns were concealed by a Bras Chapeau,
And the Devil went forth as natty a Beau
As Bond-street ever saw.

He sate him down, in London town,
Before earth's morning ray;
With a favourite imp he began to chat,
On religion, and scandal, this and that,
Until the dawn of day.

And then to St. James's Court he went,
And St. Paul's Church he took on his way;
He was mighty thick with every Saint,
Though they were formal and he was gay.

The Devil was an agriculturist,
And as bad weeds quickly grow,
In looking over his farm, I wist,
He wouldn't find cause for woe.

He peeped in each hole, to each chamber stole,
His promising live-stock to view;
Grinning applause, he just showed them his claws,

And they shrunk with affright from his ugly sight,
Whose work they delighted to do.

Satan poked his red nose into crannies so small
One would think that the innocents fair,
Poor lambkins! were just doing nothing at all
But settling some dress or arranging some ball,
But the Devil saw deeper there.

A Priest, at whose elbow the Devil during prayer
Sate familiarly, side by side,
Declared that, if the Tempter were there,
His presence he would not abide.
Ah! ah! thought Old Nick, that's a very stale trick,
For without the Devil, O favourite of Evil,
In your carriage you would not ride.

Satan next saw a brainless King,
Whose house was as hot as his own;
Many Imps in attendance were there on the wing,
They flapped the pennon and twisted the sting,
Close by the very Throne.

Ah! ah! thought Satan, the pasture is good,
My Cattle will here thrive better than others;
They dine on news of human blood,
They sup on the groans of the dying and dead,
And supperless never will go to bed;
Which will make them fat as their brothers.

Fat as the Fiends that feed on blood,
Fresh and warm from the fields of Spain,

Where Ruin ploughs her gory way,
Where the shoots of earth are nipped in the bud,
Where Hell is the Victor's prey,
Its glory the meed of the slain.

Fat—as the Death-birds on Erin's shore,
That glutted themselves in her dearest gore,
And flitted round Castlereagh,
When they snatched the Patriot's heart, that HIS grasp
Had torn from its widow's maniac clasp,
—And fled at the dawn of day.

Fat—as the Reptiles of the tomb,
That riot in corruption's spoil,
That fret their little hour in gloom,
And creep, and live the while.

Fat as that Prince's maudlin brain,
Which, addled by some gilded toy,
Tired, gives his sweetmeat, and again
Cries for it, like a humoured boy.

For he is fat,—his waistcoat gay,
When strained upon a levee day,
Scarce meets across his princely paunch;
And pantaloons are like half-moons
Upon each brawny haunch.

How vast his stock of calf! when plenty
Had filled his empty head and heart,
Enough to satiate foplings twenty,
Could make his pantaloon seams start.

The Devil (who sometimes is called Nature),
For men of power provides thus well,
Whilst every change and every feature,
Their great original can tell.

Satan saw a lawyer a viper slay,
That crawled up the leg of his table,
It reminded him most marvellously
Of the story of Cain and Abel.

The wealthy yeoman, as he wanders
His fertile fields among,
And on his thriving cattle ponders,
Counts his sure gains, and hums a song;
Thus did the Devil, through earth walking,
Hum low a hellish song.

For they thrive well whose garb of gore
Is Satan's choicest livery,
And they thrive well who from the poor
Have snatched the bread of penury,
And heap the houseless wanderer's store
On the rank pile of luxury.

The Bishops thrive, though they are big;
The Lawyers thrive, though they are thin;
For every gown, and every wig,
Hides the safe thrift of Hell within.

Thus pigs were never counted clean,
Although they dine on finest corn;

And cormorants are sin-like lean,
Although they eat from night to morn.

Oh! why is the Father of Hell in such glee,
As he grins from ear to ear?
Why does he doff his clothes joyfully,
As he skips, and prances, and flaps his wing,
As he sidles, leers, and twirls his sting,
And dares, as he is, to appear?

A statesman passed—alone to him,
The Devil dare his whole shape uncover,
To show each feature, every limb,
Secure of an unchanging lover.

At this known sign, a welcome sight,
The watchful demons sought their King,
And every Fiend of the Stygian night,
Was in an instant on the wing.

Pale Loyalty, his guilt-steeled brow,
With wreaths of gory laurel crowned:
The hell-hounds, Murder, Want and Woe,
Forever hungering, flocked around;
From Spain had Satan sought their food,
'Twas human woe and human blood!

Hark! the earthquake's crash I hear,—
Kings turn pale, and Conquerors start,
Ruffians tremble in their fear,
For their Satan doth depart.

This day Fiends give to revelry
To celebrate their King's return,
And with delight its Sire to see
Hell's adamantine limits burn.

But were the Devil's sight as keen
As Reason's penetrating eye,
His sulphurous Majesty I ween,
Would find but little cause for joy.

For the sons of Reason see
That, ere fate consume the Pole,
The false Tyrant's cheek shall be
Bloodless as his coward soul.

Mutability

The flower that smiles to-day
  To-morrow dies;
All that we wish to stay
  Tempts and then flies.
What is this world's delight?
Lightning that mocks the night,
  Brief even as bright.

Virtue, how frail it is!
  Friendship how rare!
Love, how it sells poor bliss
  For proud despair!
But we, though soon they fall,
Survive their joy, and all
  Which ours we call.

Whilst skies are blue and bright,
  Whilst flowers are gay,
Whilst eyes that change ere night
  Make glad the day;
Whilst yet the calm hours creep,
Dream thou—and from thy sleep
  Then wake to weep.

Alastor, or The Spirit of Solitude

Earth, Ocean, Air, beloved brotherhood!
If our great Mother has imbued my soul
With aught of natural piety to feel
Your love, and recompense the boon with mine;
If dewy morn, and odorous noon, and even,
With sunset and its gorgeous ministers,
And solemn midnight's tingling silentness;
If autumn's hollow sighs in the sere wood,
And winter robing with pure snow and crowns
Of starry ice the grey grass and bare boughs;
If spring's voluptuous pantings when she breathes
Her first sweet kisses, have been dear to me;
If no bright bird, insect, or gentle beast
I consciously have injured, but still loved
And cherished these my kindred; then forgive
This boast, beloved brethren, and withdraw
No portion of your wonted favour now!

Mother of this unfathomable world!
Favour my solemn song, for I have loved
Thee ever, and thee only; I have watched
Thy shadow, and the darkness of thy steps,
And my heart ever gazes on the depth
Of thy deep mysteries. I have made my bed
In charnels and on coffins, where black death
Keeps record of the trophies won from thee,
Hoping to still these obstinate questionings
Of thee and thine, by forcing some lone ghost,
Thy messenger, to render up the tale
Of what we are. In lone and silent hours,

When night makes a weird sound of its own stillness,
Like an inspired and desperate alchymist
Staking his very life on some dark hope,
Have I mixed awful talk and asking looks
With my most innocent love, until strange tears,
Uniting with those breathless kisses, made
Such magic as compels the charmed night
To render up thy charge:...and, though ne'er yet
Thou hast unveiled thy inmost sanctuary,
Enough from incommunicable dream,
And twilight phantasms, and deep noon-day thought,
Has shone within me, that serenely now
And moveless, as a long-forgotten lyre
Suspended in the solitary dome
Of some mysterious and deserted fane,
I wait thy breath, Great Parent, that my strain
May modulate with murmurs of the air,
And motions of the forests and the sea,
And voice of living beings, and woven hymns
Of night and day, and the deep heart of man.

There was a Poet whose untimely tomb
No human hands with pious reverence reared,
But the charmed eddies of autumnal winds
Built o'er his mouldering bones a pyramid
Of mouldering leaves in the waste wilderness:—
A lovely youth,—no mourning maiden decked
With weeping flowers, or votive cypress wreath,
The lone couch of his everlasting sleep:—
Gentle, and brave, and generous,—no lorn bard
Breathed o'er his dark fate one melodious sigh:
He lived, he died, he sung in solitude.

Strangers have wept to hear his passionate notes,
And virgins, as unknown he passed, have pined
And wasted for fond love of his wild eyes.
The fire of those soft orbs has ceased to burn,
And Silence, too enamoured of that voice,
Locks its mute music in her rugged cell.

By solemn vision, and bright silver dream
His infancy was nurtured. Every sight
And sound from the vast earth and ambient air,
Sent to his heart its choicest impulses.
The fountains of divine philosophy
Fled not his thirsting lips, and all of great,
Or good, or lovely, which the sacred past
In truth or fable consecrates, he felt
And knew. When early youth had passed, he left
His cold fireside and alienated home
To seek strange truths in undiscovered lands.
Many a wide waste and tangled wilderness
Has lured his fearless steps; and he has bought
With his sweet voice and eyes, from savage men,
His rest and food. Nature's most secret steps
He like her shadow has pursued, where'er
The red volcano overcanopies
Its fields of snow and pinnacles of ice
With burning smoke, or where bitumen lakes
On black bare pointed islets ever beat
With sluggish surge, or where the secret caves,
Rugged and dark, winding among the springs
Of fire and poison, inaccessible
To avarice or pride, their starry domes
Of diamond and of gold expand above

Numberless and immeasurable halls,
Frequent with crystal column, and clear shrines
Of pearl, and thrones radiant with chrysolite.
Nor had that scene of ampler majesty
Than gems or gold, the varying roof of heaven
And the green earth lost in his heart its claims
To love and wonder; he would linger long
In lonesome vales, making the wild his home,
Until the doves and squirrels would partake
From his innocuous hand his bloodless food,
Lured by the gentle meaning of his looks,
And the wild antelope, that starts whene'er
The dry leaf rustles in the brake, suspend
Her timid steps, to gaze upon a form
More graceful than her own.

         His wandering step,
Obedient to high thoughts, has visited
The awful ruins of the days of old:
Athens, and Tyre, and Balbec, and the waste
Where stood Jerusalem, the fallen towers
Of Babylon, the eternal pyramids,
Memphis and Thebes, and whatsoe'er of strange,
Sculptured on alabaster obelisk,
Or jasper tomb, or mutilated sphynx,
Dark Aethiopia in her desert hills
Conceals. Among the ruined temples there,
Stupendous columns, and wild images
Of more than man, where marble daemons watch
The Zodiac's brazen mystery, and dead men
Hang their mute thoughts on the mute walls around,
He lingered, poring on memorials

Of the world's youth: through the long burning day
Gazed on those speechless shapes; nor, when the moon
Filled the mysterious halls with floating shades
Suspended he that task, but ever gazed
And gazed, till meaning on his vacant mind
Flashed like strong inspiration, and he saw
The thrilling secrets of the birth of time.

Meanwhile an Arab maiden brought his food,
Her daily portion, from her father's tent,
And spread her matting for his couch, and stole
From duties and repose to tend his steps,
Enamoured, yet not daring for deep awe
To speak her love:—and watched his nightly sleep,
Sleepless herself, to gaze upon his lips
Parted in slumber, whence the regular breath
Of innocent dreams arose; then, when red morn
Made paler the pale moon, to her cold home
Wildered, and wan, and panting, she returned.

The Poet, wandering on, through Arabie,
And Persia, and the wild Carmanian waste,
And o'er the aerial mountains which pour down
Indus and Oxus from their icy caves,
In joy and exultation held his way;
Till in the vale of Cashmire, far within
Its loneliest dell, where odorous plants entwine
Beneath the hollow rocks a natural bower,
Beside a sparkling rivulet he stretched
His languid limbs. A vision on his sleep
There came, a dream of hopes that never yet
Had flushed his cheek. He dreamed a veiled maid

Sate near him, talking in low solemn tones.
Her voice was like the voice of his own soul
Heard in the calm of thought; its music long,
Like woven sounds of streams and breezes, held
His inmost sense suspended in its web
Of many-coloured woof and shifting hues.
Knowledge and truth and virtue were her theme,
And lofty hopes of divine liberty,
Thoughts the most dear to him, and poesy,
Herself a poet. Soon the solemn mood
Of her pure mind kindled through all her frame
A permeating fire; wild numbers then
She raised, with voice stifled in tremulous sobs
Subdued by its own pathos; her fair hands
Were bare alone, sweeping from some strange harp
Strange symphony, and in their branching veins
The eloquent blood told an ineffable tale.
The beating of her heart was heard to fill
The pauses of her music, and her breath
Tumultuously accorded with those fits
Of intermitted song. Sudden she rose,
As if her heart impatiently endured
Its bursting burthen: at the sound he turned,
And saw by the warm light of their own life
Her glowing limbs beneath the sinuous veil
Of woven wind, her outspread arms now bare,
Her dark locks floating in the breath of night,
Her beamy bending eyes, her parted lips
Outstretched, and pale, and quivering eagerly.
His strong heart sunk and sickened with excess
Of love. He reared his shuddering limbs and quelled
His gasping breath, and spread his arms to meet

Her panting bosom:...she drew back a while,
Then, yielding to the irresistible joy,
With frantic gesture and short breathless cry
Folded his frame in her dissolving arms.
Now blackness veiled his dizzy eyes, and night
Involved and swallowed up the vision; sleep,
Like a dark flood suspended in its course,
Rolled back its impulse on his vacant brain.

Roused by the shock he started from his trance—
The cold white light of morning, the blue moon
Low in the west, the clear and garish hills,
The distinct valley and the vacant woods,
Spread round him where he stood. Whither have fled
The hues of heaven that canopied his bower
Of yesternight? The sounds that soothed his sleep,
The mystery and the majesty of Earth,
The joy, the exultation? His wan eyes
Gaze on the empty scene as vacantly
As ocean's moon looks on the moon in heaven.
The spirit of sweet human love has sent
A vision to the sleep of him who spurned
Her choicest gifts. He eagerly pursues
Beyond the realms of dream that fleeting shade;
He overleaps the bounds. Alas! Alas!
Were limbs, and breath, and being intertwined
Thus treacherously? Lost, lost, for ever lost
In the wide pathless desert of dim sleep,
That beautiful shape! Does the dark gate of death
Conduct to thy mysterious paradise,
O Sleep? Does the bright arch of rainbow clouds
And pendent mountains seen in the calm lake,

Lead only to a black and watery depth,
While death's blue vault, with loathliest vapours hung,
Where every shade which the foul grave exhales
Hides its dead eye from the detested day,
Conducts, O Sleep, to thy delightful realms?
This doubt with sudden tide flowed on his heart;
The insatiate hope which it awakened, stung
His brain even like despair.

           While daylight held
The sky, the Poet kept mute conference
With his still soul. At night the passion came,
Like the fierce fiend of a distempered dream,
And shook him from his rest, and led him forth
Into the darkness.—As an eagle, grasped
In folds of the green serpent, feels her breast
Burn with the poison, and precipitates
Through night and day, tempest, and calm, and cloud,
Frantic with dizzying anguish, her blind flight
O'er the wide aery wilderness: thus driven
By the bright shadow of that lovely dream,
Beneath the cold glare of the desolate night,
Through tangled swamps and deep precipitous dells,
Startling with careless step the moonlight snake,
He fled. Red morning dawned upon his flight,
Shedding the mockery of its vital hues
Upon his cheek of death. He wandered on
Till vast Aornos seen from Petra's steep
Hung o'er the low horizon like a cloud;
Through Balk, and where the desolated tombs
Of Parthian kings scatter to every wind
Their wasting dust, wildly he wandered on,

Day after day a weary waste of hours,
Bearing within his life the brooding care
That ever fed on its decaying flame.
And now his limbs were lean; his scattered hair,
Sered by the autumn of strange suffering
Sung dirges in the wind; his listless hand
Hung like dead bone within its withered skin;
Life, and the lustre that consumed it, shone
As in a furnace burning secretly
From his dark eyes alone. The cottagers,
Who ministered with human charity
His human wants, beheld with wondering awe
Their fleeting visitant. The mountaineer,
Encountering on some dizzy precipice
That spectral form, deemed that the Spirit of wind
With lightning eyes, and eager breath, and feet
Disturbing not the drifted snow, had paused
In its career: the infant would conceal
His troubled visage in his mother's robe
In terror at the glare of those wild eyes,
To remember their strange light in many a dream
Of after-times; but youthful maidens, taught
By nature, would interpret half the woe
That wasted him, would call him with false names
Brother and friend, would press his pallid hand
At parting, and watch, dim through tears, the path
Of his departure from their father's door.

At length upon the lone Chorasmian shore
He paused, a wide and melancholy waste
Of putrid marshes. A strong impulse urged

His steps to the sea-shore. A swan was there,
Beside a sluggish stream among the reeds.
It rose as he approached, and, with strong wings
Scaling the upward sky, bent its bright course
High over the immeasurable main.
His eyes pursued its flight:—'Thou hast a home,
Beautiful bird; thou voyagest to thine home,
Where thy sweet mate will twine her downy neck
With thine, and welcome thy return with eyes
Bright in the lustre of their own fond joy.
And what am I that I should linger here,
With voice far sweeter than thy dying notes,
Spirit more vast than thine, frame more attuned
To beauty, wasting these surpassing powers
In the deaf air, to the blind earth, and heaven
That echoes not my thoughts?' A gloomy smile
Of desperate hope wrinkled his quivering lips.
For sleep, he knew, kept most relentlessly
Its precious charge, and silent death exposed,
Faithless perhaps as sleep, a shadowy lure,
With doubtful smile mocking its own strange charms.

Startled by his own thoughts he looked around.
There was no fair fiend near him, not a sight
Or sound of awe but in his own deep mind.
A little shallop floating near the shore
Caught the impatient wandering of his gaze.
It had been long abandoned, for its sides
Gaped wide with many a rift, and its frail joints
Swayed with the undulations of the tide.
A restless impulse urged him to embark

And meet lone Death on the drear ocean's waste;
For well he knew that mighty Shadow loves
The slimy caverns of the populous deep.

The day was fair and sunny; sea and sky
Drank its inspiring radiance, and the wind
Swept strongly from the shore, blackening the waves.
Following his eager soul, the wanderer
Leaped in the boat, he spread his cloak aloft
On the bare mast, and took his lonely seat,
And felt the boat speed o'er the tranquil sea
Like a torn cloud before the hurricane.

As one that in a silver vision floats
Obedient to the sweep of odorous winds
Upon resplendent clouds, so rapidly
Along the dark and ruffled waters fled
The straining boat.—A whirlwind swept it on
With fierce gusts and precipitating force,
Through the white ridges of the chafed sea.
The waves arose. Higher and higher still
Their fierce necks writhed beneath the tempest's scourge
Like serpents struggling in a vulture's grasp.
Calm and rejoicing in the fearful war
Of wave ruining on wave, and blast on blast
Descending, and black flood on whirlpool driven
With dark obliterating course, he sate:
As if their genii were the ministers
Appointed to conduct him to the light
Of those beloved eyes, the Poet sate,
Holding the steady helm. Evening came on,
The beams of sunset hung their rainbow hues

High 'mid the shifting domes of sheeted spray
That canopied his path o'er the waste deep;
Twilight, ascending slowly from the east,
Entwined in duskier wreaths her braided locks
O'er the fair front and radiant eyes of day;
Night followed, clad with stars. On every side
More horribly the multitudinous streams
Of ocean's mountainous waste to mutual war
Rushed in dark tumult thundering, as to mock
The calm and spangled sky. The little boat
Still fled before the storm; still fled, like foam
Down the steep cataract of a wintry river;
Now pausing on the edge of the riven wave;
Now leaving far behind the bursting mass
That fell, convulsing ocean: safely fled—
As if that frail and wasted human form,
Had been an elemental god.

> At midnight
The moon arose; and lo! the ethereal cliffs
Of Caucasus, whose icy summits shone
Among the stars like sunlight, and around
Whose caverned base the whirlpools and the waves
Bursting and eddying irresistibly
Rage and resound forever.—Who shall save?—
The boat fled on,—the boiling torrent drove,—
The crags closed round with black and jagged arms,
The shattered mountain overhung the sea,
And faster still, beyond all human speed,
Suspended on the sweep of the smooth wave,
The little boat was driven. A cavern there
Yawned, and amid its slant and winding depths

Ingulfed the rushing sea. The boat fled on
With unrelaxing speed.—'Vision and Love!'
The Poet cried aloud, 'I have beheld
The path of thy departure. Sleep and death
Shall not divide us long.'

The boat pursued
The windings of the cavern. Daylight shone
At length upon that gloomy river's flow;
Now, where the fiercest war among the waves
Is calm, on the unfathomable stream
The boat moved slowly. Where the mountain, riven,
Exposed those black depths to the azure sky,
Ere yet the flood's enormous volume fell
Even to the base of Caucasus, with sound
That shook the everlasting rocks, the mass
Filled with one whirlpool all that ample chasm:
Stair above stair the eddying waters rose,
Circling immeasurably fast, and laved
With alternating dash the gnarled roots
Of mighty trees, that stretched their giant arms
In darkness over it. I' the midst was left,
Reflecting, yet distorting every cloud,
A pool of treacherous and tremendous calm.
Seized by the sway of the ascending stream,
With dizzy swiftness, round, and round, and round,
Ridge after ridge the straining boat arose,
Till on the verge of the extremest curve,
Where, through an opening of the rocky bank,
The waters overflow, and a smooth spot
Of glassy quiet mid those battling tides
Is left, the boat paused shuddering.—Shall it sink

Down the abyss? Shall the reverting stress
Of that resistless gulf embosom it?
Now shall it fall?—A wandering stream of wind,
Breathed from the west, has caught the expanded sail,
And, lo! with gentle motion, between banks
Of mossy slope, and on a placid stream,
Beneath a woven grove it sails, and, hark!
The ghastly torrent mingles its far roar,
With the breeze murmuring in the musical woods.
Where the embowering trees recede, and leave
A little space of green expanse, the cove
Is closed by meeting banks, whose yellow flowers
For ever gaze on their own drooping eyes,
Reflected in the crystal calm. The wave
Of the boat's motion marred their pensive task,
Which naught but vagrant bird, or wanton wind,
Or falling spear-grass, or their own decay
Had e'er disturbed before. The Poet longed
To deck with their bright hues his withered hair,
But on his heart its solitude returned,
And he forbore. Not the strong impulse hid
In those flushed cheeks, bent eyes, and shadowy frame
Had yet performed its ministry: it hung
Upon his life, as lightning in a cloud
Gleams, hovering ere it vanish, ere the floods
Of night close over it.

        The noonday sun
Now shone upon the forest, one vast mass
Of mingling shade, whose brown magnificence
A narrow vale embosoms. There, huge caves,
Scooped in the dark base of their aery rocks,

Mocking its moans, respond and roar for ever.
The meeting boughs and implicated leaves
Wove twilight o'er the Poet's path, as led
By love, or dream, or god, or mightier Death,
He sought in Nature's dearest haunt some bank,
Her cradle, and his sepulchre. More dark
And dark the shades accumulate. The oak,
Expanding its immense and knotty arms,
Embraces the light beech. The pyramids
Of the tall cedar overarching frame
Most solemn domes within, and far below,
Like clouds suspended in an emerald sky,
The ash and the acacia floating hang
Tremulous and pale. Like restless serpents, clothed
In rainbow and in fire, the parasites,
Starred with ten thousand blossoms, flow around
The grey trunks, and, as gamesome infants' eyes,
With gentle meanings, and most innocent wiles,
Fold their beams round the hearts of those that love,
These twine their tendrils with the wedded boughs
Uniting their close union; the woven leaves
Make net-work of the dark blue light of day,
And the night's noontide clearness, mutable
As shapes in the weird clouds. Soft mossy lawns
Beneath these canopies extend their swells,
Fragrant with perfumed herbs, and eyed with blooms
Minute yet beautiful. One darkest glen
Sends from its woods of musk-rose, twined with jasmine,
A soul-dissolving odour to invite
To some more lovely mystery. Through the dell,
Silence and Twilight here, twin-sisters, keep

Their noonday watch, and sail among the shades,
Like vaporous shapes half-seen; beyond, a well,
Dark, gleaming, and of most translucent wave,
Images all the woven boughs above,
And each depending leaf, and every speck
Of azure sky, darting between their chasms;
Nor aught else in the liquid mirror laves
Its portraiture, but some inconstant star
Between one foliaged lattice twinkling fair,
Or painted bird, sleeping beneath the moon,
Or gorgeous insect floating motionless,
Unconscious of the day, ere yet his wings
Have spread their glories to the gaze of noon.

Hither the Poet came. His eyes beheld
Their own wan light through the reflected lines
Of his thin hair, distinct in the dark depth
Of that still fountain; as the human heart,
Gazing in dreams over the gloomy grave,
Sees its own treacherous likeness there. He heard
The motion of the leaves, the grass that sprung
Startled and glanced and trembled even to feel
An unaccustomed presence, and the sound
Of the sweet brook that from the secret springs
Of that dark fountain rose. A Spirit seemed
To stand beside him—clothed in no bright robes
Of shadowy silver or enshrining light,
Borrowed from aught the visible world affords
Of grace, or majesty, or mystery;—
But, undulating woods, and silent well,
And leaping rivulet, and evening gloom

Now deepening the dark shades, for speech assuming,
Held commune with him, as if he and it
Were all that was,—only...when his regard
Was raised by intense pensiveness,...two eyes,
Two starry eyes, hung in the gloom of thought,
And seemed with their serene and azure smiles
To beckon him.

Obedient to the light
That shone within his soul, he went, pursuing
The windings of the dell.—The rivulet,
Wanton and wild, through many a green ravine
Beneath the forest flowed. Sometimes it fell
Among the moss with hollow harmony
Dark and profound. Now on the polished stones
It danced; like childhood laughing as it went:
Then, through the plain in tranquil wanderings crept,
Reflecting every herb and drooping bud
That overhung its quietness.—'O stream!
Whose source is inaccessibly profound,
Whither do thy mysterious waters tend?
Thou imagest my life. Thy darksome stillness,
Thy dazzling waves, thy loud and hollow gulfs,
Thy searchless fountain, and invisible course
Have each their type in me; and the wide sky.
And measureless ocean may declare as soon
What oozy cavern or what wandering cloud
Contains thy waters, as the universe
Tell where these living thoughts reside, when stretched
Upon thy flowers my bloodless limbs shall waste
I' the passing wind!'

                    Beside the grassy shore
Of the small stream he went; he did impress
On the green moss his tremulous step, that caught
Strong shuddering from his burning limbs. As one
Roused by some joyous madness from the couch
Of fever, he did move; yet, not like him,
Forgetful of the grave, where, when the flame
Of his frail exultation shall be spent,
He must descend. With rapid steps he went
Beneath the shade of trees, beside the flow
Of the wild babbling rivulet; and now
The forest's solemn canopies were changed
For the uniform and lightsome evening sky.
Grey rocks did peep from the spare moss, and stemmed
The struggling brook; tall spires of windlestrae
Threw their thin shadows down the rugged slope,
And nought but gnarled roots of ancient pines
Branchless and blasted, clenched with grasping roots
The unwilling soil. A gradual change was here,
Yet ghastly. For, as fast years flow away,
The smooth brow gathers, and the hair grows thin
And white, and where irradiate dewy eyes
Had shone, gleam stony orbs:—so from his steps
Bright flowers departed, and the beautiful shade
Of the green groves, with all their odorous winds
And musical motions. Calm, he still pursued
The stream, that with a larger volume now
Rolled through the labyrinthine dell; and there
Fretted a path through its descending curves
With its wintry speed. On every side now rose
Rocks, which, in unimaginable forms,
Lifted their black and barren pinnacles

In the light of evening, and its precipice
Obscuring the ravine, disclosed above,
Mid toppling stones, black gulfs and yawning caves,
Whose windings gave ten thousand various tongues
To the loud stream. Lo! where the pass expands
Its stony jaws, the abrupt mountain breaks,
And seems, with its accumulated crags,
To overhang the world: for wide expand
Beneath the wan stars and descending moon
Islanded seas, blue mountains, mighty streams,
Dim tracts and vast, robed in the lustrous gloom
Of leaden-coloured even, and fiery hills
Mingling their flames with twilight, on the verge
Of the remote horizon. The near scene,
In naked and severe simplicity,
Made contrast with the universe. A pine,
Rock-rooted, stretched athwart the vacancy
Its swinging boughs, to each inconstant blast
Yielding one only response, at each pause
In most familiar cadence, with the howl
The thunder and the hiss of homeless streams
Mingling its solemn song, whilst the broad river
Foaming and hurrying o'er its rugged path,
Fell into that immeasurable void
Scattering its waters to the passing winds.

Yet the grey precipice and solemn pine
And torrent were not all;—one silent nook
Was there. Even on the edge of that vast mountain,
Upheld by knotty roots and fallen rocks,
It overlooked in its serenity
The dark earth, and the bending vault of stars.

It was a tranquil spot, that seemed to smile
Even in the lap of horror. Ivy clasped
The fissured stones with its entwining arms,
And did embower with leaves for ever green,
And berries dark, the smooth and even space
Of its inviolated floor, and here
The children of the autumnal whirlwind bore,
In wanton sport, those bright leaves, whose decay,
Red, yellow, or ethereally pale,
Rivals the pride of summer. 'Tis the haunt
Of every gentle wind, whose breath can teach
The wilds to love tranquillity. One step,
One human step alone, has ever broken
The stillness of its solitude:—one voice
Alone inspired its echoes;—even that voice
Which hither came, floating among the winds,
And led the loveliest among human forms
To make their wild haunts the depository
Of all the grace and beauty that endued
Its motions, render up its majesty,
Scatter its music on the unfeeling storm,
And to the damp leaves and blue cavern mould,
Nurses of rainbow flowers and branching moss,
Commit the colours of that varying cheek,
That snowy breast, those dark and drooping eyes.

The dim and horned moon hung low, and poured
A sea of lustre on the horizon's verge
That overflowed its mountains. Yellow mist
Filled the unbounded atmosphere, and drank
Wan moonlight even to fulness; not a star
Shone, not a sound was heard; the very winds,

Danger's grim playmates, on that precipice
Slept, clasped in his embrace.—O, storm of death!
Whose sightless speed divides this sullen night:
And thou, colossal Skeleton, that, still
Guiding its irresistible career
In thy devastating omnipotence,
Art king of this frail world, from the red field
Of slaughter, from the reeking hospital,
The patriot's sacred couch, the snowy bed
Of innocence, the scaffold and the throne,
A mighty voice invokes thee. Ruin calls
His brother Death. A rare and regal prey
He hath prepared, prowling around the world;
Glutted with which thou mayst repose, and men
Go to their graves like flowers or creeping worms,
Nor ever more offer at thy dark shrine
The unheeded tribute of a broken heart.

When on the threshold of the green recess
The wanderer's footsteps fell, he knew that death
Was on him. Yet a little, ere it fled,
Did he resign his high and holy soul
To images of the majestic past,
That paused within his passive being now,
Like winds that bear sweet music, when they breathe
Through some dim latticed chamber. He did place
His pale lean hand upon the rugged trunk
Of the old pine. Upon an ivied stone
Reclined his languid head, his limbs did rest,
Diffused and motionless, on the smooth brink
Of that obscurest chasm;—and thus he lay,

Surrendering to their final impulses
The hovering powers of life. Hope and despair,
The torturers, slept; no mortal pain or fear
Marred his repose; the influxes of sense,
And his own being unalloyed by pain,
Yet feebler and more feeble, calmly fed
The stream of thought, till he lay breathing there
At peace, and faintly smiling:—his last sight
Was the great moon, which o'er the western line
Of the wide world her mighty horn suspended,
With whose dun beams inwoven darkness seemed
To mingle. Now upon the jagged hills
It rests; and still as the divided frame
Of the vast meteor sunk, the Poet's blood,
That ever beat in mystic sympathy
With nature's ebb and flow, grew feebler still:
And when two lessening points of light alone
Gleamed through the darkness, the alternate gasp
Of his faint respiration scarce did stir
The stagnate night:—till the minutest ray
Was quenched, the pulse yet lingered in his heart.
It paused—it fluttered. But when heaven remained
Utterly black, the murky shades involved
An image, silent, cold, and motionless,
As their own voiceless earth and vacant air.
Even as a vapour fed with golden beams
That ministered on sunlight, ere the west
Eclipses it, was now that wondrous frame—
No sense, no motion, no divinity—
A fragile lute, on whose harmonious strings
The breath of heaven did wander—a bright stream

Once fed with many-voiced waves—a dream
Of youth, which night and time have quenched for ever,
Still, dark, and dry, and unremembered now.

Oh, for Medea's wondrous alchemy,
Which wheresoe'er it fell made the earth gleam
With bright flowers, and the wintry boughs exhale
From vernal blooms fresh fragrance! O, that God
Profuse of poisons, would concede the chalice
Which but one living man has drained, who now,
Vessel of deathless wrath, a slave that feels
No proud exemption in the blighting curse
He bears, over the world wanders for ever,
Lone as incarnate death! O, that the dream
Of dark magician in his visioned cave,
Raking the cinders of a crucible
For life and power, even when his feeble hand
Shakes in its last decay, were the true law
Of this so lovely world! But thou art fled,
Like some frail exhalation; which the dawn
Robes in its golden beams,—ah! thou hast fled!
The brave, the gentle and the beautiful,
The child of grace and genius. Heartless things
Are done and said i' the world, and many worms
And beasts and men live on, and mighty Earth
From sea and mountain, city and wilderness,
In vesper low or joyous orison,
Lifts still its solemn voice:—but thou art fled—
Thou canst no longer know or love the shapes
Of this phantasmal scene, who have to thee
Been purest ministers, who are, alas!
Now thou art not. Upon those pallid lips

So sweet even in their silence, on those eyes
That image sleep in death, upon that form
Yet safe from the worm's outrage, let no tear
Be shed—not even in thought. Nor, when those hues
Are gone, and those divinest lineaments,
Worn by the senseless wind, shall live alone
In the frail pauses of this simple strain,
Let not high verse, mourning the memory
Of that which is no more, or painting's woe
Or sculpture, speak in feeble imagery
Their own cold powers. Art and eloquence,
And all the shows o' the world are frail and vain
To weep a loss that turns their lights to shade.
It is a woe 'too deep for tears,' when all
Is reft at once, when some surpassing Spirit,
Whose light adorned the world around it, leaves
Those who remain behind, not sobs or groans,
The passionate tumult of a clinging hope;
But pale despair and cold tranquillity,
Nature's vast frame, the web of human things,
Birth and the grave, that are not as they were.

The Daemon of the World

Part I

Nee tantum prodere vati,
Quantum scire licet. Venit setas omms in unam
Congeriem, miserumque premunt tot saecula pectus.

Lucan Phars. L. y. L 176.

How wonderful is Death,
Death and his brother Sleep!
One pale as yonder wan and hornèd moon,
With lips of lurid blue,
The other glowing like the vital morn,
When throned on ocean's wave
It breathes over the world:
Yet both so passing strange and wonderful!

Hath then the iron-sceptred Skeleton,
Whose reign is in the tainted sepulchres,
To the hell dogs that couch beneath his throne
Cast that fair prey? Must that divinest form,
Which love and admiration cannot view
Without a beating heart, whose azure veins
Steal like dark streams along a field of snow,
Whose outline is as fair as marble clothed
In light of some sublimest mind, decay?
Nor putrefaction's breath

Leave aught of this pure spectacle
But loathsomeness and ruin?—
Spare aught but a dark theme.
On which the lightest heart might moralize?
Or is it but that downy-wingèd slumbers
Have charmed their nurse coy Silence near her lids
To watch their own repose?
Will they, when morning's beam
Flows through those wells of light,
Seek far from noise and day some western cave,

Where woods and streams with soft and pausing winds
A lulling murmur weave?—

Ianthe doth not sleep
The dreamless sleep of death:
Nor in her moonlight chamber silently,
Doth Henry hear her regular pulses throb,
Or mark her delicate cheek
With interchange of hues mock the broad moon
Outwatching weary night.
Without assured reward.
Her dewy eyes are closed;
On their translucent lids, whose testure fine
Scarce hide the dark blue orbs that burn below
With unapparent fire,
The baby Sleep is pillowed:
Her golden tresses shade
The bosom's stainless pride,
Twining like tendrils of the parasite
Around a marble column.

Hark! whence that rushing sound?
'Tis like a wondrous strain that sweeps
Around a lonely ruin
When west winds sigh and evening waves respond
In whispers from the shore:
'Tis wilder than the unmeasured notes
Which from the unseen lyres of dells and groves
The genii of the breezes sweep.
Floating on waves of music and of light
The chariot of the Dæmon of the World
Descends in silent power:
Its shape reposed within: slight as some cloud
That catches but the palest tinge of day
When evening yields to night.
Bright as that fibrous woof when stars indue
Its transitory robe.
Four shapeless shadows bright and beautiful
Draw that strange car of glory, reins of light
Check their unearthly speed; they stop and fold
Their wings of braided air:
The Dæmon leaning from the etherial car
Gazed on the slumbering maid.
Human eye hath ne'er beheld
A shape so wild, so bright, so beautiful,
As that which o'er the maiden's charmèd sleep
Waving a starry wand,
Hung like a mist of light.
Such sounds as breathed around like odorous winds
Of wakening spring arose,
Filling the chamber and the moonlight sky.

Maiden, the world's supremest spirit
Beneath the shadow of her wings
Folds all thy memory doth inherit
From ruin of divinest things,
Feelings that lure thee to betray,
And light of thoughts that pass away.

For thou hast earned a mighty boon,
The truths which wisest poets see

Dimly, thy mind may make its own,
Rewarding its own majesty,
Entranced in some diviner mood
Of self-oblivious solitude.

Custom, and Faith, and Power thou spurnest;
From hate and awe thy heart is free;
Ardent and pure as day thou burnest,
For dark and cold mortality
A living light, to cheer it long,
The watch-fires of the world among.

Therefore from nature's inner shrine,
Where gods and fiends in worship bend,
Majestic spirit, be it thine
The flame to seize, the veil to rend,
Where the vast snake Eternity
In charmèd sleep doth ever lie.

All that inspires thy voice of love,
Or speaks in thy unclosing eyes.

Or through thy frame doth burn or move,
Or think or feel, awake, arise!
Spirit, leave for mine and me
Earth's unsubstantial mimicry!

It ceased, and from the mute and moveless frame
A radiant spirit arose,
All beautiful in naked purity.
Robed in its human hues it did ascend,
Disparting as it went the silver clouds
It moved towards the car, and took its seat
Beside the Dæmon shape.

Obedient to the sweep of aery song,
The mighty ministers
Unfurled their prismy wings.
The magic car moved on;
The night was fair, innumerable stars
Studded heaven's dark blue vault;
The eastern wave grew pale
With the first smile of morn.

The magic car moved on
From the swift sweep of wings
The atmosphere in flaming sparkles flew;
And where the burning wheels
Eddied above the mountain's loftiest peak
Was traced a line of lightning.
Now far above a rock the utmost verge
Of the wide earth it flew,
The rival of the Andes, whose dark brow
Frowned o'er the silver sea.

Far, far below the chariot's stormy path,
Calm as a slumbering babe,
Tremendous ocean lay.
Its broad and silent mirror gave to view
The pale and waning stars,
The chariot's fiery track,
And the grey light of morn
Tinging those fleecy clouds
That cradled in their folds the infant dawn.

The chariot seemed to fly
Through the abyss of an immense concave,
Radiant with million constellations, tinged
With shades of infinite colour,
And semicircled with a belt
Flashing incessant meteors.

As they approached their goal,
The wingèd shadows seemed to gather speed.
The sea no longer was distinguished; earth
Appeared a vast and shadowy sphere, suspended
In the black concave of heaven
With the sun's cloudless orb,
Whose rays of rapid light
Parted around the chariot's swifter course,
And fell like ocean's feathery spray
Dashed from the boiling surge
Before a vessel's prow.

The magic car moved on.
Earth's distant orb appeared

The smallest light that twinkles in the heavens,
Whilst round the chariot's way
Innumerable systems widely rolled,
And countless spheres diffused
An ever varying glory.
It was a sight of wonder! Some were horned,
And, like the moon's argentine crescent hung
In the dark dome of heaven, some did shed
A clear mild beam like Hesperus, while the sea
Yet glows with fading sun-light; others dashed
Athwart the night with trains of bickering fire.
Like spherèd worlds to death and ruin driven;
Some shone like stars, and as the chariot passed
Bedimmed all other light

Spirit of Nature! here
In this interminable wilderness
Of worlds, at whose involved immensity
Even soaring fancy staggers,
Here is thy fitting temple.

Yet not the lightest leaf
That quivers to the passing breeze
Is less instinct with thee,—
Yet not the meanest worm,
That lurks in graves and fattens on the dead
Less shares thy eternal breath.
Spirit of Nature! thou
Imperishable as this glorious scene,
Here is thy fitting temple.

If solitude hath ever led thy steps
To the shore of the immeasurable sea,
And thou hast lingered there
Until the sun's broad orb
Seemed resting on the fiery line of ocean,
Thou must have marked the braided webs of gold
That without motion hang
Over the sinking sphere:
Thou must have marked the billowy mountain clouds,
Edged with intolerable radiancy,

Towering like rocks of jet
Above the burning deep:
And yet there is a moment
When the sun's highest point
Peers like a star o'er ocean's western edge,
When those far clouds of feathery purple gleam
Like fairy lands girt by some heavenly sea:
Then has thy rapt imagination soared
Where in the midst of all existing things
The temple of the mightiest Dæmon stands.

Yet not the golden islands
That gleam amid yon flood of purple light,
Nor the feathery curtains
That canopy the sun's resplendent couch,
Nor the burnished ocean waves
Paving that gorgeous dome.
So fair, so wonderful a sight
As the eternal temple could afford.
The elements of all that human thought

Can frame of lovely or sublime, did join
To rear the fabric of the fane, nor aught
Of earth may image forth its majesty.
Yet likest evening's vault that faëry hall,
As heaven low resting on the wave it spread
Its floors of flashing light,
Its vast and azure dome;
And on the verge of that obscure abyss
Where crystal battlements o'erhang the gulph
Of the dark world, ten thousand spheres diffuse
Their lustre through its adamantine gates.

The magic car no longer moved;
The Dæmon and the Spirit
Entered the eternal gates.
Those clouds of aery gold
That slept in glittering billows
Beneath the azure canopy,
With the etherial footsteps trembled not;
While slight and odorous mists

Floated to strains of thrilling melody
Through the vast columns and the pearly shrines.

The Dæmon and the Spirit
Approached the overhanging battlement.
Below lay stretched the boundless universe!
There, far as the remotest line
That limits swift imagination's flight,
Unending orbs mingled in mazy motion,
Immutably fulfilling

Eternal Nature's law.
Above, below, around,
The circling systems formed
A wilderness of harmony,
Each with undeviating aim
In eloquent silence through the depths of space
Pursued its wondrous way.—

Awhile the Spirit paused in ecstasy.
Yet soon she saw, as the vast spheres swept by,

Strange things within their belted orbs appear.
Like animated frenzies, dimly moved
Shadows, and skeletons, and fiendly shapes,
Thronging round human graves, and o'er the dead
Sculpturing records for each memory
In verse, such as malignant gods pronounce,
Blasting the hopes of men, when heaven and hell
Confounded burst in ruin o'er the world:
And they did build vast trophies, instruments
Of murder, human bones, barbaric gold,
Skins torn from living men, and towers of skulls
With sightless holes gazing on blinder heaven,
Mitres, and crowns, and brazen chariots stained
With blood, and scrolls of mystic wickedness,
The sanguine codes of venerable crime.
The likeness of a thronèd king came by,
When these had past, bearing upon his brow
A threefold crown; his countenance was calm,
His eye severe and cold; but his right hand
Was charged with bloody coin, and he did gnaw

By fits, with secret smiles, a human heart
Concealed beneath his robe; and motley shapes,
A multitudinous throng, around him knelt,
With bosoms bare, and bowed heads, and false looks
Of true submission, as the sphere rolled by,
Brooking no eye to witness their foul shame,
Which human hearts must feel, while human tongues
Tremble to speak, they did rage horribly,
Breathing in self contempt fierce blasphemies
Against the Dæmon of the World, and high
Hurling their armèd hands where the pure Spirit,
Serene and inaccessibly secure,
Stood on an isolated pinnacle,
The flood of ages combating below
The depth of the unbounded universe
Above, and all around
Necessity's unchanging harmony.

Part II

O happy Earth! reality of Heaven!
To which those restless powers that ceaselessly
Throng through the human universe, aspire;
Thou consummation of all mortal hope!
Thou glorious prize of blindly-working will!
Whose rays, diffused throughout all space and time,
Verge to one point and blend forever there:
Of purest spirits thou pure dwelling-place!
Where care and sorrow, impotence and crime,
Languor, disease, and ignorance dare not come:
happy Earth, reality of Heaven!

Genius has seen thee in her passionate dreams.
And dim forebodings of thy loveliness
Haunting the human heart, have there entwined

Those rooted hopes, that the proud Power of Evil
Shall not forever on this fairest world
Shake pestilence and war, or that his slaves
With blasphemy for prayer, and human blood
For sacrifice, before his shrine forever
In adoration bend, or Erebus
With all its banded fiends shall not uprise
To overwhelm in envy and revenge
The dauntless and the good, who dare to hurl
Defiance at his throne, girt tho' it be
With Death's omnipotence. Thou hast beheld
His empire, o'er the present and the past;
It was a desolate sight—now gaze on mine,
Futurity. Thou hoary giant Time,
Render thou up thy half-devoured babes,—
And from the cradles of eternity,
Where millions lie lulled to their portioned sleep
By the deep murmuring stream of passing things,
Tear thou that gloomy shroud.—Spirit, behold
Thy glorious destiny!

The Spirit saw
The vast frame of the renovated world
Smile in the lap of Chaos, and the sense
Of hope thro' her fine texture did suffuse
Such varying glow, as summer evening casts
On undulating clouds and deepening lakes.
Like the vague sighings of a wind at even,

That wakes the wavelets of the slumbering sea
And dies on the creation of its breath.
And sinks and rises, fails and swells by fits:
Was the sweet stream of thought that with wild motion
Flowed o'er the Spirit's human sympathies.
The mighty tide of thought had paused awhile,
Which from the Dæmon now like Ocean's stream
Again began to pour.—

To me is given
The wonders of the human world to keep—
Space, matter, time and mind—let the sight
Renew and strengthen all thy failing hope.

All things are recreated, and the flame
Of consentaneous love inspires all life:
The fertile bosom of the earth gives suck
To myriads, who still grow beneath her care.
Rewarding her with their pure perfectness:
The balmy breathings of the wind inhale
Her virtues, and diffuse them all abroad:
Health floats amid the gentle atmosphere.
Glows in the fruits, and mantles on the stream
No storms deform the beaming brow of heaven.
Nor scatter in the freshness of its pride
The foliage of the undecaying trees;
But fruits are ever ripe, flowers ever fair,
And Autumn proudly bears her matron grace,
Kindling a flush on the fair cheek of Spring,
Whose virgin bloom beneath the ruddy fruit
Reflects its tint and blushes into love

The habitable earth is full of bliss;
Those wastes of frozen billows that were hurled

By everlasting snow-storms round the poles,
Where matter dared nor vegetate nor live,
But ceaseless frost round the vast solitude
Bound its broad zone of stillness, are unloosed;
And fragrant zephyrs there from spicy isles
Ruffle the placid ocean-deep, that rolls
Its broad, bright surges to the sloping sand.
Whose roar is wakened into echoings sweet
To murmur through the heaven-breathing groves
And melodize with man's blest nature there.

The vast tract of the parched and sandy waste
Now teems with countless rills and shady woods,
Corn-fields and pastures and white cottages;
And where the startled wilderness did hear
A savage conqueror stained in kindred blood,
Hymning his victory, or the milder snake
Crushing the bones of some frail antelope
Within his brazen folds—the dewy lawn.
Offering sweet incense to the sun-rise, smiles

To see a babe before his mother's door.
Share with the green and golden basilisk
That comes to lick his feet, his morning's meal.

Those trackless deeps, where many a weary sail
Has seen above the illimitable plain,
Morning on night, and night on morning rise,

Whilst still no land to greet the wanderer spread
Its shadowy mountains on the sun-bright sea,
Where the loud roarings of the tempest-waves
So long have mingled with the gusty wind
In melancholy loneliness, and swept
The desert of those ocean solitudes,
But vocal to the sea-bird's harrowing shriek,
The bellowing monster, and the rushing storm.
Now to the sweet and many-mingling sounds
Of kindliest human impulses respond:
Those lonely realms bright garden-isles begem,
With lightsome clouds and shining seas between,
And fertile vallies, resonant with bliss,

Whilst green woods overcanopy the wave,
Which like a toil-worn labourer leaps to shore,
To meet the kisses of the flowrets there.

Man chief perceives the change, his being notes
The gradual renovation, and defines
Each movement of its progress on his mind.
Man, where the gloom of the long polar night
Lowered o'er the snow-clad rocks and frozen soil,
Where scarce the hardest herb that braves the frost
Basked in the moonlight's ineffectual glow,
Shrank with the plants, and darkened with the night;
Nor where the tropics bound the realms of day
With a broad belt of mingling cloud and flame,
Where blue mists through the unmoving atmosphere
Scattered the seeds of pestilence, and fed
Unnatural vegetation, where the land
Teemed with all earthquake, tempest and disease,

Was man a nobler being; slavery
Had crushed him to his country's bloodstained dust.

Even where the milder zone afforded man
A seeming shelter, yet contagion there,
Blighting his being with unnumbered ills,
Spread like a quenchless fire; nor truth availed
Till late to arrest its progress, or create
That peace which first in bloodless victory waved
Her snowy standard o'er this favoured clime:
There man was long the train-bearer of slaves.
The mimic of surrounding misery.
The jackal of ambition's lion-rage.
The bloodhound of religion's hungry zeal.

Here now the human being stands adorning
This loveliest earth with taintless body and mind;
Blest from his birth with all bland impulses.
Which gently in his noble bosom wake
All kindly passions and all pure desires.
Him, still from hope to hope the bliss pursuing,
Which from the exhaustless lore of human weal
Draws on the virtuous mind, the thoughts that rise

In time-destroying infiniteness, gift
With self-enshrined eternity, that mocks
The unprevailing hoariness of age,
And man, once fleeting o'er the transient scene
Swift as an unremembered vision, stands
Immortal upon earth: no longer now
He slays the beast that sports around his dwelling
And horribly devours its mangled flesh.

Or drinks its vital blood, which like a stream
Of poison thro' his fevered veins did flow
Feeding a plague that secretly consumed
His feeble frame, and kindling in his mind
Hatred, despair, and fear and vain belief.
The germs of misery, death, disease, and crime.
No longer now the winged habitants,
That in the woods their sweet lives sing away,
Flee from the form of man; but gather round,
And prune their sunny feathers on the hands
Which little children stretch in friendly sport
Towards these dreadless partners of their play.

All things are void of terror: man has lost
His desolating privilege, and stands
An equal amidst equals: happiness
And science dawn though late upon the earth;
Peace cheers the mind, health renovates the frame;
Disease and pleasure cease to mingle here,
Reason and passion cease to combat there;
Whilst mind unfettered o'er the earth extends
Its all-subduing energies, and wields
The sceptre of a vast dominion there.

Mild is the slow necessity of death:
The tranquil spirit fails beneath its grasp.
Without a groan, almost without a fear,
Resigned in peace to the necessity,
Calm as a voyager to some distant land.
And full of wonder, full of hope as he.
The deadly germs of languor and disease

Waste in the human frame, and Nature gifts
With choicest boons her human worshippers.

How vigorous now the athletic form of age!
How clear its open and unwrinkled brow!
Where neither avarice, cunning, pride, or care,
Had stamped the seal of grey deformity
On all the mingling lineaments of time.
How lovely the intrepid front of youth !
How sweet the smiles of taintless infancy.

Within the massy prison's mouldering courts.
Fearless and free the ruddy children play,
Weaving gay chaplets for their innocent brows
With the green ivy and the red wall-flower,
That mock the dungeon's unavailing gloom;
The ponderous chains, and gratings of strong iron.
There rust amid the accumulated ruins
Now mingling slowly with their native earth:
There the broad beam of day, which feebly once
Lighted the cheek of lean captivity
With a pale and sickly glare, now freely shines
On the pure smiles of infant playfulness:
No more the shuddering voice of hoarse despair
Peals through the echoing vaults, but soothing notes
Of ivy-fingered winds and gladsome birds
And merriment are resonant around.

The fanes of Fear and Falsehood hear no more
The voice that once waked multitudes to war
Thundering thro' all their aisles: but now respond

To the death dirge of the melancholy wind:
It were a sight of awfulness to see
The works of faith and slavery, so vast,
So sumptuous, yet withal so perishing!
Even as the corpse that rests beneath their wall.
A thousand mourners deck the pomp of death
To-day, the breathing marble glows above
To decorate its memory, and tongues
Are busy of its life: to-morrow, worms
In silence and in darkness seize their prey.
These ruins soon leave not a wreck behind:
Their elements, wide scattered o'er the globe.

To happier shapes are moulded, and become
Ministrant to all blissful impulses:
Thus human things are perfected, and earth,
Even as a child beneath its mother's love,
Is strengthened in all excellence, and grows
Fairer and nobler with each passing year.

Now Time his dusky pennons o'er the scene
Closes in steadfast darkness, and the past
Fades from our charmèd sight. My task is done:
Thy lore is learned. Earth's wonders are thine own,
With all the fear and all the hope they bring.
My spells are past: the present now recurs.
Ah me! a pathless wilderness remains
Yet unsubdued by man's reclaiming hand.

Yet, human Spirit, bravely hold thy course,
Let virtue teach thee firmly to pursue
The gradual paths of an aspiring change:

For birth and life and death, and that strange state
Before the naked powers that thro' the world
Wander like winds have found a human home,
All tend to perfect happiness, and urge
The restless wheels of being on their way,
Whose flashing spokes, instinct with infinite life,
Bicker and burn to gain their destined goal:
For birth but wakes the universal mind

Whose mighty streams might else in silence flow
Thro' the vast world, to individual sense
Of outward shews, whose unexperienced shape
New modes of passion to its frame may lend;
Life is its state of action, and the store
Of all events is aggregated there
That variegate the eternal universe;
Death is a gate of dreariness and gloom,
That leads to azure isles and beaming skies
And happy regions of eternal hope.
Therefore, O Spirit! fearlessly bear on:
Though storms may break the primrose on its stalk,
Though frosts may blight the freshness of its bloom,

Yet spring's awakening breath will woo the earth,
To feed with kindliest dews its favourite flower,
That blooms in mossy banks and darksome glens,
Lighting the green wood with its sunny smile.

Fear not then, Spirit, death's disrobing hand.
So welcome when the tyrant is awake.
So welcome when the bigot's hell-torch flares;
'Tis but the voyage of a darksome hour.

The transient gulph-dream of a startling sleep.
For what thou art shall perish utterly,
But what is thine may never cease to be;
Death is no foe to virtue: earth has seen
Love's brightest roses on the scaffold bloom,
Mingling with freedom's fadeless laurels there,
And presaging the truth of visioned bliss.
Are there not hopes within thee, which this
   scene
Of linked and gradual being has confirmed?
Hopes that not vainly thou, and living fires
Of mind, as radiant and as pure as thou

Have shone upon the paths of men—return
Surpassing Spirit, to that world, where thou
Art destined an eternal war to wage
With tyranny and falsehood, and uproot
The germs of misery from the human heart.
Thine is the hand whose piety would soothe
The thorny pillow of unhappy crime.
Whose impotence an easy pardon gains,
Watching its wanderings as a friend's disease:
Thine is the brow whose mildness would defy
Its fiercest rage, and brave its sternest will,
When fenced by power and master of the world.
Thou art sincere and good; of resolute mind,
Free from heart-withering custom's cold control.
Of passion lofty, pure and unsubdued.
Earth's pride and meanness could not vanquish
   thee,
And therefore art thou worthy of the boon
Which thou hast now received: virtue shall keep

Thy footsteps in the path that thou hast trod.
And many days of beaming hope shall bless

Thy spotless life of sweet and sacred love.
Go, happy one, and give that bosom joy
Whose sleepless spirit waits to catch
Light, life and rapture from thy smile.

The Dæmon called its winged ministers.
Speechless with bliss the Spirit mounts the car,
That rolled beside the crystal battlement.
Bending her beamy eyes in thankfulness.
The burning wheels inflame
The steep descent of Heaven's untrodden way.
Fast and far the chariot flew:
The mighty globes that rolled
Around the gate of the Eternal Fane
Lessened by slow degrees, and soon appeared
Such tiny twinklers as the planet orbs
That ministering on the solar power
With borrowed light pursued their narrower way.
Earth floated then below:
The chariot paused a moment;

The Spirit then descended:
And from the earth departing
The shadows with swift wings
Speeded like thought upon the light of Heaven.

The Body and the Soul united then,
A gentle start convulsed Ianthe's frame:
Her veiny eyelids quietly unclosed;

Moveless awhile the dark blue orbs remained:
She looked around in wonder and beheld
Henry, who kneeled in silence by her couch.
Watching her sleep with looks of speechless love.
And the bright beaming stars
That through the casement shone.

Mont Blanc

I

The everlasting universe of things
Flows through the mind, and rolls its rapid waves,
Now dark—now glittering—now reflecting gloom—
Now lending splendour, where from secret springs
The source of human thought its tribute brings
Of waters,—with a sound but half its own,
Such as a feeble brook will oft assume
In the wild woods, among the mountains lone,
Where waterfalls around it leap for ever,
Where woods and winds contend, and a vast river
Over its rocks ceaselessly bursts and raves.

II

Thus thou, Ravine of Arve—dark, deep Ravine—
Thou many-coloured, many-voicèd vale,
Over whose pines, and crags, and caverns sail
Fast cloud-shadows and sunbeams: awful scene,
Where Power in likeness of the Arve comes down
From the ice-gulfs that gird his secret throne,
Bursting through these dark mountains like the flame
Of lightning through the tempest;—thou dost lie,
Thy giant brood of pines around thee clinging,
Children of elder time, in whose devotion
The chainless winds still come and ever came
To drink their odours, and their mighty swinging
To hear—an old and solemn harmony;
Thine earthly rainbows stretched across the sweep
Of the aethereal waterfall, whose veil
Robes some unsculptured image; the strange sleep

Which when the voices of the desert fail
Wraps all in its own deep eternity;—
Thy caverns echoing to the Arve's commotion,
A loud, lone sound no other sound can tame;
Thou art pervaded with that ceaseless motion,
Thou art the path of that unresting sound—
Dizzy Ravine! and when I gaze on thee
I seem as in a trance sublime and strange
To muse on my own separate fantasy,
My own, my human mind, which passively
Now renders and receives fast influencings,
Holding an unremitting interchange
With the clear universe of things around;
One legion of wild thoughts, whose wandering wings
Now float above thy darkness, and now rest
Where that or thou art no unbidden guest,
In the still cave of the witch Poesy,
Seeking among the shadows that pass by
Ghosts of all things that are, some shade of thee,
Some phantom, some faint image; till the breast
From which they fled recalls them, thou art there!

III

Some say that gleams of a remoter world
Visit the soul in sleep,—that death is slumber,
And that its shapes the busy thoughts outnumber
Of those who wake and live.—I look on high;
Has some unknown omnipotence unfurled
The veil of life and death? or do I lie
In dream, and does the mightier world of sleep
Spread far around and inaccessibly
Its circles? For the very spirit fails,

Driven like a homeless cloud from steep to steep
That vanishes among the viewless gales!
Far, far above, piercing the infinite sky,
Mont Blanc appears,—still, snowy, and serene—
Its subject mountains their unearthly forms
Pile around it, ice and rock; broad vales between
Of frozen floods, unfathomable deeps,
Blue as the overhanging heaven, that spread
And wind among the accumulated steeps;
A desert peopled by the storms alone,
Save when the eagle brings some hunter's bone,
And the wolf tracks her there—how hideously
Its shapes are heaped around! rude, bare, and high,
Ghastly, and scarred, and riven.—Is this the scene
Where the old Earthquake-daemon taught her young
Ruin? Were these their toys? or did a sea
Of fire envelop once this silent snow?
None can reply—all seems eternal now.
The wilderness has a mysterious tongue
Which teaches awful doubt, or faith so mild,
So solemn, so serene, that man may be,
But for such faith, with nature reconciled;
Thou hast a voice, great Mountain, to repeal
Large codes of fraud and woe; not understood
By all, but which the wise, and great, and good
Interpret, or make felt, or deeply feel.

IV

The fields, the lakes, the forests, and the streams,
Ocean, and all the living things that dwell
Within the daedal earth; lightning, and rain,
Earthquake, and fiery flood, and hurricane.

The torpor of the year when feeble dreams
Visit the hidden buds, or dreamless sleep
Holds every future leaf and flower;—the bound
With which from that detested trance they leap;
The works and ways of man, their death and birth,
And that of him and all that his may be;
All things that move and breathe with toil and sound
Are born and die; revolve, subside, and swell.
Power dwells apart in its tranquillity,
Remote, serene, and inaccessible:
And this, the naked countenance of earth,
On which I gaze, even these primaeval mountains
Teach the adverting mind. The glaciers creep
Like snakes that watch their prey, from their far fountains,
Slow rolling on; there, many a precipice,
Frost and the Sun in scorn of mortal power
Have piled: dome, pyramid, and pinnacle,
A city of death, distinct with many a tower
And wall impregnable of beaming ice.
Yet not a city, but a flood of ruin
Is there, that from the boundaries of the sky
Rolls its perpetual stream; vast pines are strewing
Its destined path, or in the mangled soil
Branchless and shattered stand; the rocks, drawn down
From yon remotest waste, have overthrown
The limits of the dead and living world,
Never to be reclaimed. The dwelling-place
Of insects, beasts, and birds, becomes its spoil;
Their food and their retreat for ever gone,
So much of life and joy is lost. The race
Of man flies far in dread; his work and dwelling
Vanish, like smoke before the tempest's stream,

And their place is not known. Below, vast caves
Shine in the rushing torrents' restless gleam,
Which from those secret chasms in tumult welling
Meet in the vale, and one majestic River,
The breath and blood of distant lands, for ever
Rolls its loud waters to the ocean-waves,
Breathes its swift vapours to the circling air.

V

Mont Blanc yet gleams on high:—the power is there,
The still and solemn power of many sights,
And many sounds, and much of life and death.
In the calm darkness of the moonless nights,
In the lone glare of day, the snows descend
Upon that Mountain; none beholds them there,
Nor when the flakes burn in the sinking sun,
Or the star-beams dart through them:—Winds contend
Silently there, and heap the snow with breath
Rapid and strong, but silently! Its home
The voiceless lightning in these solitudes
Keeps innocently, and like vapour broods
Over the snow. The secret Strength of things
Which governs thought, and to the infinite dome
Of Heaven is as a law, inhabits thee!
And what were thou, and earth, and stars, and sea,
If to the human mind's imaginings
Silence and solitude were vacancy?

Satan Broken Loose

A golden-winged Angel stood
Before the Eternal Judgement-seat:
His looks were wild, and Devils' blood
Stained his dainty hands and feet.
The Father and the Son
Knew that strife was now begun.
They knew that Satan had broken his chain,
And with millions of daemons in his train,
Was ranging over the world again.
Before the Angel had told his tale,
A sweet and a creeping sound
Like the rushing of wings was heard around;
And suddenly the lamps grew pale —
The lamps, before the Archangels seven,
That burn continually in Heaven.

The Vine Shroud

Flourishing vine, whose kindling clusters glow
Beneath the autumnal sun, none taste of thee;
For thou dost shroud a ruin, and below
The rotting bones of dead antiquity.

Ozymandias

I met a traveller from an antique land
Who said:—Two vast and trunkless legs of stone
Stand in the desert. Near them on the sand,
Half sunk, a shatter'd visage lies, whose frown
And wrinkled lip and sneer of cold command
Tell that its sculptor well those passions read
Which yet survive, stamp'd on these lifeless things,
The hand that mock'd them and the heart that fed.
And on the pedestal these words appear:
'My name is Ozymandias, king of kings:
Look on my works, ye mighty, and despair!'
Nothing beside remains: round the decay
Of that colossal wreck, boundless and bare,
The lone and level sands stretch far away.

Music

I pant for the music which is divine,
My heart in its thirst is a dying flower;
Pour forth the sound like enchanted wine,
Loosen the notes in a silver shower;
Like a herbless plain, for the gentle rain,
I gasp, I faint, till they wake again.

Let me drink of the spirit of that sweet sound,
More, oh more,—I am thirsting yet;
It loosens the serpent which care has bound
Upon my heart to stifle it;
The dissolving strain, through every vein,
Passes into my heart and brain.

As the scent of a violet withered up,
Which grew by the brink of a silver lake,
When the hot noon has drained its dewy cup,
And mist there was none its thirst to slake—
And the violet lay dead while the odour flew
On the wings of the wind o'er the waters blue—

As one who drinks from a charmed cup
Of foaming, and sparkling, and murmuring wine,
Whom, a mighty Enchantress filling up,
Invites to love with her kiss divine...

Ode to Naples

Epode 1a

I stood within the City disinterred;
And heard the autumnal leaves like light footfalls
Of spirits passing through the streets; and heard
The Mountain's slumberous voice at intervals
Thrill through those roofless halls;
The oracular thunder penetrating shook
The listening soul in my suspended blood;
I felt that Earth out of her deep heart spoke—
I felt, but heard not:—through white columns glowed
The isle-sustaining ocean-flood,
A plane of light between two heavens of azure!
Around me gleamed many a bright sepulchre
Of whose pure beauty, Time, as if his pleasure
Were to spare Death, had never made erasure;
But every living lineament was clear
As in the sculptor's thought; and there
The wreaths of stony myrtle, ivy, and pine,
Like winter leaves o'ergrown by moulded snow,
Seemed only not to move and grow
Because the crystal silence of the air
Weighed on their life; even as the Power divine
Which then lulled all things, brooded upon mine.

Epode 2a

Then gentle winds arose
With many a mingled close
Of wild Aeolian sound, and mountain-odours keen;
And where the Baian ocean
Welters with airlike motion,

Within, above, around its bowers of starry green,
Moving the sea-flowers in those purple caves,
Even as the ever stormless atmosphere
Floats o'er the Elysian realm,
It bore me, like an Angel, o'er the waves
Of sunlight, whose swift pinnace of dewy air
No storm can overwhelm.
I sailed, where ever flows
Under the calm Serene
A spirit of deep emotion
From the unknown graves
Of the dead Kings of Melody.
Shadowy Aornos darkened o'er the helm
The horizontal aether; Heaven stripped bare
Its depth over Elysium, where the prow
Made the invisible water white as snow;
From that Typhaean mount, Inarime,
There streamed a sunbright vapour, like the standard
Of some aethereal host;
Whilst from all the coast,
Louder and louder, gathering round, there wandered
Over the oracular woods and divine sea
Prophesyings which grew articulate—
They seize me—I must speak them!—be they fate!

Strophe 1

Naples! thou Heart of men which ever pantest
Naked, beneath the lidless eye of Heaven!
Elysian City, which to calm enchantest
The mutinous air and sea! they round thee, even
As sleep round Love, are driven!
Metropolis of a ruined Paradise

Long lost, late won, and yet but half regained!
Bright Altar of the bloodless sacrifice
Which armed Victory offers up unstained
To Love, the flower-enchained!
Thou which wert once, and then didst cease to be,
Now art, and henceforth ever shalt be, free,
If Hope, and Truth, and Justice can avail,—
Hail, hail, all hail!

Strophe 2
Thou youngest giant birth
Which from the groaning earth
Leap'st, clothed in armour of impenetrable scale!
Last of the Intercessors!
Who 'gainst the Crowned Transgressors
Pleadest before God's love! Arrayed in Wisdom's mail,
Wave thy lightning lance in mirth
Nor let thy high heart fail,
Though from their hundred gates the leagued Oppressors
With hurried legions move!
Hail, hail, all hail!

Antistrophe 1a
What though Cimmerian Anarchs dare blaspheme
Freedom and thee? thy shield is as a mirror
To make their blind slaves see, and with fierce gleam
To turn his hungry sword upon the wearer;
A new Actaeon's error
Shall theirs have been—devoured by their own hounds!
Be thou like the imperial Basilisk
Killing thy foe with unapparent wounds!
Gaze on Oppression, till at that dread risk

Aghast she pass from the Earth's disk:
Fear not, but gaze—for freemen mightier grow,
And slaves more feeble, gazing on their foe:—
If Hope, and Truth, and Justice may avail,
Thou shalt be great—All hail!

Antistrophe 2a

From Freedom's form divine,
From Nature's inmost shrine,
Strip every impious gawd, rend
Error veil by veil;
O'er Ruin desolate,
O'er Falsehood's fallen state,
Sit thou sublime, unawed; be the Destroyer pale!
And equal laws be thine,
And winged words let sail,
Freighted with truth even from the throne of God:
That wealth, surviving fate,
Be thine.—All hail!

Antistrophe 1b

Didst thou not start to hear Spain's thrilling paean
From land to land re-echoed solemnly,
Till silence became music? From the Aeaean
To the cold Alps, eternal Italy
Starts to hear thine! The Sea
Which paves the desert streets of Venice laughs
In light, and music; widowed Genoa wan
By moonlight spells ancestral epitaphs,
Murmuring, 'Where is Doria?' fair Milan,
Within whose veins long ran
The viper's palsying venom, lifts her heel

To bruise his head. The signal and the seal
(If Hope and Truth and Justice can avail)
Art thou of all these hopes.—O hail!

Antistrophe 2b

Florence! beneath the sun,
Of cities fairest one,
Blushes within her bower for Freedom's expectation:
From eyes of quenchless hope
Rome tears the priestly cope,
As ruling once by power, so now by admiration,—
An athlete stripped to run
From a remoter station
For the high prize lost on Philippi's shore:—
As then Hope, Truth, and Justice did avail,
So now may Fraud and Wrong! O hail!

Epode 1b

Hear ye the march as of the Earth-born Forms
Arrayed against the ever-living Gods?
The crash and darkness of a thousand storms
Bursting their inaccessible abodes
Of crags and thunder-clouds?
See ye the banners blazoned to the day,
Inwrought with emblems of barbaric pride?
Dissonant threats kill Silence far away,
The serene Heaven which wraps our Eden wide
With iron light is dyed;
The Anarchs of the North lead forth their legions
Like Chaos o'er creation, uncreating;
An hundred tribes nourished on strange religions
And lawless slaveries,—down the aereal regions

Of the white Alps, desolating,
Famished wolves that bide no waiting,
Blotting the glowing footsteps of old glory,
Trampling our columned cities into dust,
Their dull and savage lust
On Beauty's corse to sickness satiating—
They come! The fields they tread look black and hoary
With fire—from their red feet the streams run gory!

Epode 2b

Great Spirit, deepest Love!
Which rulest and dost move
All things which live and are, within the Italian shore;
Who spreadest Heaven around it,
Whose woods, rocks, waves, surround it;
Who sittest in thy star, o'er Ocean's western floor;
Spirit of beauty! at whose soft command
The sunbeams and the showers distil its foison
From the Earth's bosom chill;
Oh, bid those beams be each a blinding brand
Of lightning! bid those showers be dews of poison!
Bid the Earth's plenty kill!
Bid thy bright Heaven above,
Whilst light and darkness bound it,
Be their tomb who planned
To make it ours and thine!
Or, with thine harmonising ardours fill
And raise thy sons, as o'er the prone horizon
Thy lamp feeds every twilight wave with fire—
Be man's high hope and unextinct desire
The instrument to work thy will divine!
Then clouds from sunbeams, antelopes from leopards,

And frowns and fears from thee,
Would not more swiftly flee
Than Celtic wolves from the Ausonian shepherds.—
Whatever, Spirit, from thy starry shrine
Thou yieldest or withholdest, oh, let be
This city of thy worship ever free!

Love's Philosophy

The fountains mingle with the river,
And the rivers with the ocean;
The winds of heaven mix for ever,
With a sweet emotion;
Nothing in the world is single;
All things by a law divine
In one another's being mingle:—
Why not I with thine?

See, the mountains kiss high heaven
And the waves clasp one another;
No sister flower would be forgiven
If it disdain'd its brother:
And the sunlight clasps the earth,
And the moonbeams kiss the sea:—
What is all this sweet work worth,
If thou kiss not me?

Time Long Past

Like the ghost of a dear friend dead
Is Time long past.
A tone which is now forever fled,
A hope which is now forever past,
A love so sweet it could not last,
Was Time long past.

There were sweet dreams in the night
Of Time long past:
And, was it sadness or delight,
Each day a shadow onward cast
Which made us wish it yet might last—
That Time long past.

There is regret, almost remorse,
For Time long past.
'Tis like a child's beloved corse
A father watches, till at last
Beauty is like remembrance, cast
From Time long past.

Good-night

Good-night? ah! no; the hour is ill
Which severs those it should unite;
Let us remain together still,
Then it will be good night.

How can I call the lone night good,
Though thy sweet wishes wing its flight?
Be it not said, thought, understood—
Then it will be—good night.

To hearts which near each other move
From evening close to morning light,
The night is good; because, my love,
They never say good-night.

A Dream of the Unknown

I dream'd that as I wander'd by the way
Bare winter suddenly was changed to spring,
And gentle odours led my steps astray,
Mix'd with a sound of waters murmuring
Along a shelving bank of turf, which lay
Under a copse, and hardly dared to fling
Its green arms round the bosom of the stream,
But kiss'd it and then fled, as thou mightest in dream.

There grew pied wind-flowers and violets,
Daisies, those pearl'd Arcturi of the earth,
The constellated flower that never sets;
Faint oxlips; tender bluebells, at whose birth
The sod scarce heaved; and that tall flower that wets—
Like a child, half in tenderness and mirth—
Its mother's face with heaven-collected tears,
When the low wind, its playmate's voice, it hears.

And in the warm hedge grew lush eglantine,
Green cow-bind and the moonlight-colour'd may,
And cherry-blossoms, and white cups, whose wine
Was the bright dew yet drain'd not by the day;
And wild roses, and ivy serpentine
With its dark buds and leaves, wandering astray;
And flowers azure, black, and streak'd with gold,
Fairer than any waken'd eyes behold.

And nearer to the river's trembling edge
There grew broad flag-flowers, purple prank'd with white,
And starry river-buds among the sedge,

And floating water-lilies, broad and bright,
Which lit the oak that overhung the hedge
With moonlight beams of their own watery light;
And bulrushes, and reeds of such deep green
As soothed the dazzled eye with sober sheen.

Methought that of these visionary flowers
I made a nosegay, bound in such a way
That the same hues, which in their natural bowers
Were mingled or opposed, the like array
Kept these imprison'd children of the Hours
Within my hand,—and then, elate and gay,
I hasten'd to the spot whence I had come
That I might there present it—oh! to Whom?

A Vision of the Sea

'Tis the terror of tempest. The rags of the sail
Are flickering in ribbons within the fierce gale:
From the stark night of vapours the dim rain is driven,
And when lightning is loosed, like a deluge from heaven,
She sees the black trunks of the water-spouts spin,
And bend, as if heaven was raining in,
Which they seem'd to sustain with their terrible mass
As if ocean had sank from beneath them: they pass
To their graves in the deep with an earthquake of sound,
And the waves and the thunders made silent around
Leave the wind to its echo. The vessel, now toss'd
Through the low-trailing rack of the tempest, is lost
In the skirts of the thunder-cloud: now down the sweep
Of the wind-cloven wave to the chasm of the deep
It sinks, and the walls of the watery vale
Whose depths of dread calm are unmoved by the gale,
Dim mirrors of ruin hang gleaming about;
While the surf, like a chaos of stars, like a rout
Of death-flames, like whirlpools of fire-flowing iron
With splendour and terror the black ship environ,
Or like sulphur-flakes hurl'd from a mine of pale fire
In fountains spout o'er it. In many a spire
The pyramid-billows with white points of brine
In the cope of the lightning inconstantly shine,
As piercing the sky from the floor of the sea.
The great ship seems splitting! it cracks as a tree,
While an earthquake is splintering its root, ere the blast
Of the whirlwind that stripped it of branches has past.
The intense thunder-balls which are raining from heaven
Have shatter'd its mast, and it stands black and riven.

The chinks suck destruction. The heavy dead hulk
On the living sea rolls an inanimate bulk,
Like a corpse on the clay which is hung'ring to fold
Its corruption around it. Meanwhile, from the hold,
One deck is burst up from the waters below,
And it splits like the ice when the thaw-breezes blow
O'er the lakes of the desert! Who sit on the other?
Is that all the crew that lie burying each other,
Like the dead in a breach, round the foremast? Are those
Twin tigers, who burst, when the waters arose,
In the agony of terror, their chains in the hold;
(What now makes them tame, is what then made them
     bold;)
Who crouch, side by side, and have driven, like a crank,
The deep grip of their claws through the vibrating plank.
Are these all? Nine weeks the tall vessel had lain
On the windless expanse of the watery plain,
Where the death-darting sun cast no shadow at noon,
And there seem'd to be fire in the beams of the moon,
Till a lead-colour'd fog gather'd up from the deep
Whose breath was quick pestilence; then, the cold sleep
Crept, like blight through the ears of a thick field of corn,
O'er the populous vessel. And even and morn,
With their hammocks for coffins the seamen aghast
Like dead men the dead limbs of their comrades cast
Down the deep, which closed on them above and around,
And the sharks and the dog-fish their grave-clothes
     unbound,
And were glutted like Jews with this manna rain'd down
From God on their wilderness. One after one
The mariners died; on the eve of this day,
When the tempest was gathering in cloudy array,

But seven remain'd. Six the thunder has smitten,
And they lie black as mummies on which Time has
    written
His scorn of the embalmer; the seventh, from the deck
An oak-splinter pierced through his breast and his back,
And hung out to the tempest, a wreck on the wreck.
No more? At the helm sits a woman more fair
Than heaven, when, unbinding its star-braided hair,
It sinks with the sun on the earth and the sea.
She clasps a bright child on her upgather'd knee,
It laughs at the lightning, it mocks the mixed thunder
Of the air and the sea, with desire and with wonder
It is beckoning the tigers to rise and come near,
It would play with those eyes where the radiance of fear
Is outshining the meteors; its bosom beats high,
The heart-fire of pleasure has kindled its eye;
Whilst its mother's is lustreless. 'Smile not, my child,
'But sleep deeply and sweetly, and so be beguiled
'Of the pang that awaits us, whatever that be,
'So dreadful since thou must divide it with me!
'Dream, sleep! This pale bosom, thy cradle and bed,
'Will it rock thee not, infant? 'Tis beating with dread!
'Alas! what is life, what is death, what are we,
'That when the ship sinks we no longer may be?
'What! to see thee no more, and to feel thee no more?
'To be after life what we have been before?
'Not to touch those sweet hands? Not to look on those
    eyes.
'Those lips, and that hair, all that smiling disguise
'Thou yet wearest, sweet spirit, which I, day by day,
'Have so long called my child, but which now fades away
'Like a rainbow, and I the fallen shower?' Lo! the ship

Is settling, it topples, the leeward ports dip;
The tigers leap up when they feel the slow brine
Crawling inch by inch on them, hair, ears, limbs, and
   eyne,
Stand rigid with horror; a loud, long, hoarse cry
Bursts at once from their vitals tremendously,
And 'tis borne down the mountainous vale of the wave,
Rebounding, like thunder, from crag to cave,
Mixed with the clash of the lashing rain,
Hurried on by the might of the hurricane:
The hurricane came from the west, and past on
By the path of the gate of the eastern sun,
Transversely dividing the stream of the storm;
As an arrowy serpent, pursuing the form
Of an elephant, bursts through the brakes of the waste.
Black as a cormorant the screaming blast,
Between ocean and heaven, like an ocean, past,
Till it came to the clouds on the verge of the world
Which, based on the sea and to heaven upcurl'd,
Like columns and walls did surround and sustain
The dome of the tempest; it rent them in twain,
As a flood rends its barriers of mountainous crag:
And the dense clouds in many a ruin and rag,
Like the stones of a temple ere earthquake has past,
Like the dust of its fall, on the whirlwind are cast;
They are scatter'd like foam on the torrent; and where
The wind has burst out from the chasm, from the air
Of clear morning, the beams of the sunrise flow in,
Unimpeded, keen, golden, and crystalline,
Banded armies of light and of air; at one gate
They encounter, but interpenetrate.
And that breach in the tempest is widening away,

And the caverns of clouds are torn up by the day,
And the fierce winds are sinking with weary wings
Lulled by the motion and murmurings,
And the long glassy heave of the rocking sea,
And over head glorious, but dreadful to see
The wrecks of the tempest, like vapours of gold,
Are consuming in sunrise. The heaped waves behold
The deep calm of blue heaven dilating above,
And, like passions made still by the presence of Love,
Beneath the clear surface reflecting it slide
Tremulous with soft influence; extending its tide
From the Andes to Atlas, round mountain and isle,
Round sea-birds and wrecks, paved with heaven's azure
  smile.
The wide world of waters is vibrating. Where
Is the ship? On the verge of the wave where it lay
One tiger is mingled in ghastly affray
With a sea-snake. The foam and the smoke of the battle
Stain the clear air with sunbows; the jar, and the rattle
Of solid bones crush'd by the infinite stress
Of the snake's adamantine voluminousness;
And the hum of the hot blood that spouts and rains
Where the gripe of the tiger has wounded the veins,
Swollen with rage, strength, and effort; the whirl and the
  splash
As of some hideous engine whose brazen teeth smash
The thin winds and soft waves into thunder; the screams
And hissings crawl fast o'er the smooth ocean streams,
Each sound like a centipede. Near this commotion,
A blue shark is hanging within the blue ocean,
The fin-winged tomb of the victor. The other
Is winning his way from the fate of his brother,

To his own with the speed of despair. Lo! a boat
Advances; twelve rowers with the impulse of thought
Urge on the keen keel, the brine foams. At the stern
Three marksmen stand levelling. Hot bullets burn
In the breast of the tiger, which yet bears him on
To his refuge and ruin. One fragment alone,
'Tis dwindling and sinking, 'tis now almost gone,
Of the wreck of the vessel peers out of the sea.
With her left hand she grasps it impetuously,
With her right she sustains her fair infant. Death, Fear,
Love, Beauty, are mixed in the atmosphere;
Which trembles and burns with the fervour of dread
Around her wild eyes, her bright hand, and her head,
Like a meteor of light o'er the waters! her child
Is yet smiling, and playing, and murmuring; so smiled
The false deep ere the storm. Like a sister and brother
The child and the ocean still smile on each other,
Whilst—

Ode to Liberty

A Glorious people vibrated again
The lightning of the nations: Liberty,
From heart to heart, from tower to tower, o'er Spain,
Scattering contagious fire into the sky,
Gleamed. My soul spruned the chains of its dismay.
And, in the rapid plumes of song,
Clothed itself sublime and strong;
As a young eagle soars the morning clouds among,
Hovering inverse o'er its accustomed prey;
Till from its station in the heaven of fame
The Spirit's whirlwind rapt it, and the ray
Of the remotest sphere of living flame
Which paves the void, was from behind it flung,
As foam from a ship's swiftness, when there came
A voice out of the deep; I will record the same.

'The Sun and the serenest Moon sprang forth;
The burning stars of the abyss were hurl'd
Into the depths of heaven. The daedal earth,
That island in the ocean of the world,
Hung in its cloud of all-sustaining air;
But this divinest universe
Was yet a chaos and a curse,
For thou wert not; but power from worst producing
  worst,
The spirit of the beasts was kindled there,
And of the birds, and of the watery forms,
And there was war among them and despair
Withn them, raging without truce or terms;
The bosom of their violated nurse

Groaned, for beasts warned on beasts, and worms on
  worms,
And men on men; each beast was as a hell of storms.

'Man, the imperial shape, then multiplied
His generations under the pavilion
Of the Sun's throne: palace and pyramid,
Temple and prison, to many a swarming million,
Were, as to mountain-wolves their ragged caves.
This human living multitude
Was savage, cunning, blind, and rude,
For thou wert not; but o'er the populous solitude,
Like one fierce cloud over a waste of waves,
Hung tyranny; beneath, sate deified
The sister-pest, congregator of slaves;
Into the shadow of her pinions wide,
Anarchs and priests who feed on gold and blood,
Till with the stain their inmost souls are dyed,
Drove the astonished herds of men from every side.

'The nodding promontories, and blue isles,
And cloud-like mountains, and dividious waves
Of Greece, basked glorious in the open smiles
Of favouring heaven; from their enchanted caves
Prophetic echoes flung dim melody
On the unapprehensive wild.
The vine, the corn, the olive mild,
Grew, savage yet, to human use unreconciled;
And like the unfolded flowers beneath the sea,
Like the man's thought dark in the infant's brain,
Like aught that is which wraps what is to be,
Art's deathless dreams lay veiled by many a vein

Of Parian stone; and yet a speechless child,
Verse murmured, and Philosophy did strain
Her lidless eyes for thee; when o'er the Aegean main

'Athens arose; a city such as vision
Builds from the purple crags and silver towers
Of battlemented cloud, as in derision
Of kingliest masonry; the ocean floors
Pave it; the evening sky pavilions it;
Its portals are inhabited
By thunder-zoned winds, each head
Within its cloudy wings with sun-fire garlanded,
A divine work! Athens diviner yet
Gleamed with its crest of columns, on the will
Of man, as on a mount of diamond, set;
For thou wert, and thine all-creative skill
Peopled, with forms that mock the eternal dead
In marble immortality, that hill
Which was thine earliest throne and latest oracle.

'Within the surface of Time's fleeting river
Its wrinkled image lies, as then it lay
Immovable unquiet, and for ever
It trembles, but it cannot pass away!
The voices of thy bards and sages thunder
With an earth-awakening blast
Through the caverns of the past;
Religion veils her eyes; Oppression shrinks aghast;
A winged sound of joy and love, and wonder,
Which soars where Expectation never flew,
Rending the veil of space and time asunder!
One ocean feeds the clouds, and streams, and dew;

One sun illumines heaven; one spirit vast
With life and love makes chaos ever new,
As Athens doth the world with thy delight renew.

'Then Rome was, and from thy deep bosom fairest,
Like a wolf-cub from a Cadmaean Maenad,
She drew the milk of greatness, though thy dearest
From that Elysian food was yet unweaned;
And many a deed of terrible uprightness
By thy sweet love was sanctified;
And in thy smile, and by thy side,
Saintly Camillus lived, and firm Atilius died.
But when tears stained thy robe of vestal whiteness,
And gold profaned they Capitolian throne,
Thou didst desert, with spirit-winged lightness,
The senate of the tyrant; they sunk prone
Slaves of one tyrant. Palatinus sighed
Faint echoes of Ionian song; that tone
Thou didst delay to hear, lamenting to disown.

'From what Hyrcanian glen or frozen hill,
Or piny promontory of the Arctic main,
Or utmost islet inaccessible,
Didst thou lament the ruin of thy reign,
Teaching the woods and waves, and desert rocks,
And every Naiad's ice-cold urn,
To talk in echoes sad and stern,
Of that sublimest lore which man had dared unlearn
For neither didst thou watch the wizard flocks
Of the Scald's dreams, nor haunt the Druid's sleep,
What if the tears rained through thy shattered locks,
Were quickly dried? for thou didst groan, nor weep,

When from the sea of death to kill and burn,
The Galilean serpent forth did creep,
And made thy world an undistinguishable heap.

'A thousand years the Earth cried 'Where art thou?'
And then the shadow of thy coming fell
On Saxon Alfred's olive-cinctured brow;
And many a warrior-peopled citadel,
Like rocks, which fire lifts out of the flat deep,
Arose in sacred Italy,
Frowning o'er the tempestuous sea
Of kings and priests, and slaves, in tower-crowned
    majesty;
That multitudinous anarchy did sweep,
And burst around their walls like idle foam,
Whilst from the human spirit's deepest deep,
Strange melody with love and awe struck dumb
Dissonant arms; and Art which cannot die,
With divine want traced on our earthly home
Fit imagery to pave heaven's ever-lasting dome.

'Thou huntress swifter than the Moon! thou terror
Of the world's wolves! thou bearer of the quiver,
Whose sunlike shafts pierce tempest-winged Error,
As light may pierce the clouds when they discover
In the calm regions of the orient day!
Luther caught thy wakening glance;
Like lightning from his leaden lance
Reflected, it dissolved the visions of the trance
In which, as in a tomb, the nations lay;
And England's prophets hailed thee as their queen,
In songs whose music cannot pass away,

Though it must flow for ever; not unseen
Before the spirit-sighted countenance
Of Milton didst thou pass, from the sad scene
Beyond whose night he saw, with a dejected mien.

'The eager hours and unreluctant years
As on a dawn-illumined mountain stood,
Trampling to silence their loud hopes and fears,
Darkening each other with their multitude,
And cried aloud, 'Liberty!' Indignation
Answered Pity from her cave;
Death grew pale within the grave,
And desolation howled to the destroyer, 'Save!'
When, like heaven's son, girt by the exhalation
Of its own glorious light, thou didst arise,
Chasing thy foes from nation unto nation
Like shadows; as if day had cloven the skies
At dreaming midnight o'er the Western wave,
Men started, staggering with a glad surprise,
Under the lightnings of thine familiar eyes.

'Thou heaven of earth! what spells could pall thee then,
In ominous eclipse? A thousand years,
Bred from the slime of deep oppression's den,
Dyed all thy liquid light with blood and tears,
Till thy sweet stars could weep the stain away;
How like Bacchanals of blood
Round France, the ghastly vintage, stood
Destruction's sceptred slaves, and Folly's mitred brood!
When one, like them, but mightier far than they,
The Anarch of thine own bewildered powers,
Rose; armies mingled in obscure array,

Like clouds with clouds, darkening the sacred bowers
Of serene heaven. He, by the past pursued,
Rests with those dead but unforgotten hours,
Whose ghosts scare victor kings in their ancestral towers.

'England yet sleeps; was she not called of old?
Spain calls her now, as with its thrilling thunder
Vesuvius wakens Aetna, and the cold
Snow-crags by its reply are cloven in sunder;
O'er the lit waves every Aeolian isle
From Pithecusa to Pelorus
Howls, and leaps, and glares in chorus;
They cry, 'Be dim, ye lamps of heaven suspended o'er us,'
Her chains are threads of gold, she need but smile
And they dissolve; but Spain's were links like steel,
Till bit to dust by virtue's keenest file.
Twins of single destiny! appeal
To the eternal years enthroned before us,
In the dim West; impress us from a seal,
All ye have thought and done!
Time cannot dare conceal.

'Tomb of Arminius! render up thy dead
Till, like a standard from a watch-tower's staff,
His soul may stream over the tyrant's head!
Thy victory shall be his epitaph,
Wild Bacchanal of truth's mysterious wine,
King-deluded Germany,
His dead spirit lives in thee.
Why do we fear or hope? thou art already free!
And thou, lost Paradise of this divine
And glorious world! thou flowery wilderness!

Thou island of eternity! thou shrine
Where desolation, clothed with loveliness,
Worships the thing thou were! O Italy,
Gather thy blood into thy heart; repress
The beasts who make their dens thy sacred palaces.

'O that the free would stamp the impious name
Of 'King' into the dust; or write it there,
So that this blot upon the page of fame
Were as serpent's path, which the light air
Erases, and the flat sands close behind!
Ye the oracle have heard;
Lift the victory-flashing sword,
And cut the snaky knots of this foul Gordian word,
Which, weak itself as stubble, yet can bind
Into a mass, irrefragably firm,
The axes and the rods which awe mankind;
The sound has poison in it, 'tis the sperm
Of what makes life foul, cankerous, and abhorred;
Disdain not thou, at thine appointed term,
To set thine armed heel on this reluctant worm.

'O that the wise from their bright minds would kindle
Such lambs within the dome of this dim world,
That the pale name of Priest might shrink and dwindle
Into the hell from which it first was hurled,
A scoff of impious pride from fiends impure,
Till human thoughts might kneel alone,
Each before the judgment-throne
Of its own aweless soul, or of the power unknown!
O that the words which make the thoughts obscure
From which they spring, as clouds of glimmering dew

From a white lake blot heaven's blue portraiture,
Were stript of their thin masks and various hue,
And frowns and smiles and splendours not their own,
Till in the nakeness of false and true
They stand before their Lord, each to receive its due.

'He who taught man to vanquish whatsoever
Can be between the cradle and the grave,
Crowned him the King of Life. O vain endeavour!
If on his own high will, a willing slave,
He has enthroned the oppression and the oppressor.
What if earth can clothe and feed
Amplest millions at their need,
And power in thought be as the tree within the seed?
Or what if Art, an ardent intercessor,
Diving on fiery wings to Nature's throne,
Checks the great mother stooping to caress her,
And cries, 'Give me, thy child, dominion
Over all height and depth?' if Life can breed
New wants, and wealth from those who toil and groan,
Rend of thy gifts and hers a thousandfold for one.

'Come thou, but lead out of the inmost cave
Of man's deep spirit, as the Morning Star
Beckons the Sun from the Eoan wave,
Wisdom. I hear the pennons of her car
Self-moving like cloud charioted by flame;
Comes she not, and come ye not,
Rulers of eternal thought,
To judge with solemn truth life's ill-apportioned lot?
Blind Love, and equal Justice, and the Fame
Of what has been, the Hope of what will be?

O, Liberty! if such could be thy name
Wert thou disjoined from these, or they from thee;
If thine or theirs were treasures to be bought
By blood or tears, have not the wise and free
Wept tears, and blood like tears?'
The solemn harmony

Paused, and the spirit of that might singing
To its abyss was suddenly withdrawn;
Then as a wild swan, when sublimely winging
Its path athwart the thunder-smoke of dawn,
Sinks headlong through the aerial golden light
On the heavy sounding plain,
When the bolt has pierced its brain;
As summer clouds dissolve unburthened of their rain;
As a far taper fades with fading night;
As a brief insect dies with dying day,
My song, its pinions disarrayed of might,
Drooped; o'er it closed the echoes far away
Of the great voice which did its flight sustain,
As waves which lately paved his watery way
Hiss round a drowner's head in their tempestuous play.

Ode to the West Wind

I

O, wild West Wind, thou breath of Autumn's being,
Thou, from whose unseen presence the leaves dead
Are driven, like ghosts from an enchanter fleeing,
Yellow, and black, and pale, and hectic red,
Pestilence-stricken multitudes: O, thou,
Who chariotest to their dark wintry bed

The winged seeds, where they lie cold and low,
Each like a corpse within its grave, until
Thine azure sister of the spring shall blow

Her clarion o'er the dreaming earth, and fill
(Driving sweet buds like flocks to feed in air)
With living hues and odours plain and hill:

Wild Spirit, which art moving every where;
Destroyer and preserver; hear, O, hear!

II

Thou on whose stream, 'mid the steep sky's commotion,
Loose clouds like earth's decaying leaves are shed,
Shook from the tangled boughs of Heaven and Ocean,

Angels of rain and lightning: there are spread
On the blue surface of thine airy surge,
Like the bright hair uplifted from the head
Of some fierce Mænad, even from the dim verge
Of the horizon to the zenith's height
The locks of the approaching storm. Thou dirge

Of the dying year, to which this closing night
Will be the dome of a vast sepulchre,
Vaulted with all thy congregated might

Of vapours, from whose solid atmosphere
Black rain, and fire, and hail will burst: O, hear!

III

Thou who didst waken from his summer dreams
The blue Mediterranean, where he lay,
Lulled by the coil of his crystalline streams,

Beside a pumice isle in Baiæ's bay,
And saw in sleep old palaces and towers
Quivering within the wave's intenser day,

All overgrown with azure moss and flowers
So sweet, the sense faints picturing them! Thou
For whose path the Atlantic's level powers
Cleave themselves into chasms, while far below
The sea-blooms and the oozy woods which wear
The sapless foliage of the ocean, know

Thy voice, and suddenly grow grey with fear,
And tremble and despoil themselves: O, hear!

IV

If I were a dead leaf thou mightest bear;
If I were a swift cloud to fly with thee;
A wave to pant beneath thy power, and share

The impulse of thy strength, only less free

Than thou, O, uncontrollable! If even
I were as in my boyhood, and could be

The comrade of thy wanderings over heaven,
As then, when to outstrip thy skiey speed
Scarce seemed a vision; I would ne'er have striven

As thus with thee in prayer in my sore need.
Oh! lift me as a wave, a leaf, a cloud!
I fall upon the thorns of life! I bleed!
A heavy weight of hours has chained and bowed
One too like thee: tameless, and swift, and proud.

V

Make me thy lyre, even as the forest is:
What if my leaves are falling like its own!
The tumult of thy mighty harmonies

Will take from both a deep, autumnal tone,
Sweet though in sadness. Be thou, spirit fierce,
My spirit! Be thou me, impetuous one!

Drive my dead thoughts over the universe
Like withered leaves to quicken a new birth!
And, by the incantation of this verse,

Scatter, as from an unextinguished hearth
Ashes and sparks, my words among mankind!
Be through my lips to unawakened earth

The trumpet of a prophecy! O, wind,
If Winter comes, can Spring be far behind?

The Sensitive Plant

I

A Sensitive Plant in a garden grew,
And the young winds fed it with silver dew,
And it opened its fan-like leaves to the light,
And closed them beneath the kisses of night.

And the Spring arose on the garden fair,
Like the Spirit of Love felt every where;
And each flower and herb on Earth's dark breast
Rose from the dreams of its wintry rest.

But none ever trembled and panted with bliss
In the garden, the field, or the wilderness,
Like a doe in the noon-tide with love's sweet want,
As the companionless Sensitive Plant.

The snow-drop, and then the violet,
Arose from the ground with warm rain wet,
And their breath was mixed with fresh odour, sent
From the turf, like the voice and the instrument.

Then the pied wind-flowers and the tulip tall,
And narcissi, the fairest among them all,
Who gaze on their eyes in the stream's recess,
Till they die of their own dear loveliness;

And the Naiad-like lily of the vale,
Whom youth makes so fair and passion so pale,
That the light of its tremulous bells is seen
Through their pavilions of tender green;

And the hyacinth purple, and white, and blue,
Which flung from its bells a sweet peal anew
Of music so delicate, soft, and intense,
It was felt like an odour within the sense;

And the rose like a nymph to the bath addressed,
Which unveiled the depth of her glowing breast,
Till, fold after fold, to the fainting air
The soul of her beauty and love lay bare:

And the wand-like lily, which lifted up,
As a Maenad, its moonlight-coloured cup,
Till the fiery star, which is its eye,
Gazed through clear dew on the tender sky;

And the jessamine faint, and the sweet tuberose,
The sweetest flower for scent that blows;
And all rare blossoms from every clime
Grew in that garden in perfect prime.

And on the stream whose inconstant bosom
Was pranked, under boughs of embowering blossom,
With golden and green light, slanting through
Their heaven of many a tangled hue,

Broad water-lilies lay tremulously,
And starry river-buds glimmered by,
And around them the soft stream did glide and dance
With a motion of sweet sound and radiance.

And the sinuous paths of lawn and of moss,
Which led through the garden along and across,

Some open at once to the sun and the breeze,
Some lost among bowers of blossoming trees,

Were all paved with daisies and delicate bells
As fair as the fabulous asphodels,
And flow'rets which, drooping as day drooped too,
Fell into pavilions, white, purple, and blue,
To roof the glow-worm from the evening dew.

And from this undefiled Paradise
The flowers (as an infant's awakening eyes
Smile on its mother, whose singing sweet
Can first lull, and at last must awaken it),

When Heaven's blithe winds had unfolded them,
As mine-lamps enkindle a hidden gem,
Shone smiling to Heaven, and every one
Shared joy in the light of the gentle sun;

For each one was interpenetrated
With the light and the odour its neighbour shed,
Like young lovers whom youth and love make dear
Wrapped and filled by their mutual atmosphere.

But the Sensitive Plant which could give small fruit
Of the love which it felt from the leaf to the root,
Received more than all, it loved more than ever,
Where none wanted but it, could belong to the giver, –

For the Sensitive Plant has no bright flower;
Radiance and odour are not its dower;

It loves, even like Love, its deep heart is full,
It desires what it has not, the Beautiful!

The light winds which from unsustaining wings
Shed the music of many murmurings;
The beams which dart from many a star
Of the flowers whose hues they bear afar;

The plumed insects swift and free,
Like golden boats on a sunny sea,
Laden with light and odour, which pass
Over the gleam of the living grass;

The unseen clouds of the dew, which lie
Like fire in the flowers till the sun rides high,
Then wander like spirits among the spheres,
Each cloud faint with the fragrance it bears;

The quivering vapours of dim noontide,
Which like a sea o'er the warm earth glide,
In which every sound, and odour, and beam,
Move, as reeds in a single stream;

Each and all like ministering angels were
For the Sensitive Plant sweet joy to bear,
Whilst the lagging hours of the day went by
Like windless clouds o'er a tender sky.

And when evening descended from Heaven above,
And the Earth was all rest, and the air was all love,
And delight, though less bright, was far more deep,
And the day's veil fell from the world of sleep,

And the beasts, and the birds, and the insects were
   drowned
In an ocean of dreams without a sound;
Whose waves never mark, though they ever impress
The light sand which paves it, consciousness;

(Only overhead the sweet nightingale
Ever sang more sweet as the day might fail,
And snatches of its Elysian chant
Were mixed with the dreams of the Sensitive Plant);—

The Sensitive Plant was the earliest
Upgathered into the bosom of rest;
A sweet child weary of its delight,
The feeblest and yet the favourite,
Cradled within the embrace of Night.

II

There was a Power in this sweet place,
An Eve in this Eden; a ruling Grace
Which to the flowers, did they waken or dream,
Was as God is to the starry scheme.

A Lady, the wonder of her kind,
Whose form was upborne by a lovely mind
Which, dilating, had moulded her mien and motion
Like a sea-flower unfolded beneath the ocean,

Tended the garden from morn to even:
And the meteors of that sublunar Heaven,
Like the lamps of the air when Night walks forth,
Laughed round her footsteps up from the Earth!

She had no companion of mortal race,
But her tremulous breath and her flushing face
Told, whilst the morn kissed the sleep from her eyes,
That her dreams were less slumber than Paradise:

As if some bright Spirit for her sweet sake
Had deserted Heaven while the stars were awake,
As if yet around her he lingering were,
Though the veil of daylight concealed him from her.

Her step seemed to pity the grass it pressed;
You might hear by the heaving of her breast,
That the coming and going of the wind
Brought pleasure there and left passion behind.

And wherever her aery footstep trod,
Her trailing hair from the grassy sod
Erased its light vestige, with shadowy sweep,
Like a sunny storm o'er the dark green deep.

I doubt not the flowers of that garden sweet
Rejoiced in the sound of her gentle feet;
I doubt not they felt the spirit that came
From her glowing fingers through all their frame.

She sprinkled bright water from the stream
On those that were faint with the sunny beam;
And out of the cups of the heavy flowers
She emptied the rain of the thunder-showers.

She lifted their heads with her tender hands,
And sustained them with rods and osier-bands;

If the flowers had been her own infants, she
Could never have nursed them more tenderly.

And all killing insects and gnawing worms,
And things of obscene and unlovely forms,
She bore, in a basket of Indian woof,
Into the rough woods far aloof,—

In a basket, of grasses and wild-flowers full,
The freshest her gentle hands could pull
For the poor banished insects, whose intent,
Although they did ill, was innocent.

But the bee and the beamlike ephemeris
Whose path is the lightning's, and soft moths that kiss
The sweet lips of the flowers, and harm not, did she
Make her attendant angels be.

And many an antenatal tomb,
Where butterflies dream of the life to come,
She left clinging round the smooth and dark
Edge of the odorous cedar bark.

This fairest creature from earliest Spring
Thus moved through the garden ministering
Mi the sweet season of Summertide,
And ere the first leaf looked brown—she died!

III

Three days the flowers of the garden fair,
Like stars when the moon is awakened, were,

Or the waves of Baiae, ere luminous
She floats up through the smoke of Vesuvius.

And on the fourth, the Sensitive Plant
Felt the sound of the funeral chant,
And the steps of the bearers, heavy and slow,
And the sobs of the mourners, deep and low;

The weary sound and the heavy breath,
And the silent motions of passing death,
And the smell, cold, oppressive, and dank,
Sent through the pores of the coffin-plank;

The dark grass, and the flowers among the grass,
Were bright with tears as the crowd did pass;
From their sighs the wind caught a mournful tone,
And sate in the pines, and gave groan for groan.

The garden, once fair, became cold and foul,
Like the corpse of her who had been its soul,
Which at first was lovely as if in sleep,
Then slowly changed, till it grew a heap
To make men tremble who never weep.

Swift Summer into the Autumn flowed,
And frost in the mist of the morning rode,
Though the noonday sun looked clear and bright,
Mocking the spoil of the secret night.

The rose-leaves, like flakes of crimson snow,
Paved the turf and the moss below.

The lilies were drooping, and white, and wan,
Like the head and the skin of a dying man.

And Indian plants, of scent and hue
The sweetest that ever were fed on dew,
Leaf by leaf, day after day,
Were massed into the common clay.

And the leaves, brown, yellow, and gray, and red,
And white with the whiteness of what is dead,
Like troops of ghosts on the dry wind passed;
Their whistling noise made the birds aghast.

And the gusty winds waked the winged seeds,
Out of their birthplace of ugly weeds,
Till they clung round many a sweet flower's stem,
Which rotted into the earth with them.

The water-blooms under the rivulet
Fell from the stalks on which they were set;
And the eddies drove them here and there,
As the winds did those of the upper air.

Then the rain came down, and the broken stalks
Were bent and tangled across the walks;
And the leafless network of parasite bowers
Massed into ruin; and all sweet flowers.

Between the time of the wind and the snow
All loathliest weeds began to grow,
Whose coarse leaves were splashed with many a speck,
Like the water-snake's belly and the toad's back.

And thistles, and nettles, and darnels rank,
And the dock, and henbane, and hemlock dank,
Stretched out its long and hollow shank,
And stifled the air till the dead wind stank.

And plants, at whose names the verse feels loath,
Filled the place with a monstrous undergrowth,
Prickly, and pulpous, and blistering, and blue,
Livid, and starred with a lurid dew.

And agarics, and fungi, with mildew and mould
Started like mist from the wet ground cold;
Pale, fleshy, as if the decaying dead
With a spirit of growth had been animated!

Spawn, weeds, and filth, a leprous scum,
Made the running rivulet thick and dumb,
And at its outlet flags huge as stakes
Dammed it up with roots knotted like water-snakes.

And hour by hour, when the air was still,
The vapours arose which have strength to kill;
At morn they were seen, at noon they were felt,
At night they were darkness no star could melt.

And unctuous meteors from spray to spray
Crept and flitted in broad noonday
Unseen; every branch on which they alit
By a venomous blight was burned and bit.

The Sensitive Plant, like one forbid,
Wept, and the tears within each lid

Of its folded leaves, which together grew,
Were changed to a blight of frozen glue.

For the leaves soon fell, and the branches soon
By the heavy axe of the blast were hewn;
The sap shrank to the root through every pore
As blood to a heart that will beat no more.

For Winter came: the wind was his whip:
One choppy finger was on his lip:
He had torn the cataracts from the hills
And they clanked at his girdle like manacles;

His breath was a chain which without a sound
The earth, and the air, and the water bound;
He came, fiercely driven, in his chariot-throne
By the tenfold blasts of the Arctic zone.

Then the weeds which were forms of living death
Fled from the frost to the earth beneath.
Their decay and sudden flight from frost
Was but like the vanishing of a ghost!

And under the roots of the Sensitive Plant
The moles and the dormice died for want:
The birds dropped stiff from the frozen air
And were caught in the branches naked and bare.

First there came down a thawing rain
And its dull drops froze on the boughs again;
Then there steamed up a freezing dew
Which to the drops of the thaw-rain grew;

And a northern whirlwind, wandering about
Like a wolf that had smelt a dead child out,
Shook the boughs thus laden, and heavy, and stiff,
And snapped them off with his rigid griff.

When Winter had gone and Spring came back
The Sensitive Plant was a leafless wreck;
But the mandrakes, and toadstools, and docks, and darnels,
Rose like the dead from their ruined charnels.

IV

Whether the Sensitive Plant, or that
Which within its boughs like a Spirit sat,
Ere its outward form had known decay,
Now felt this change, I cannot say.
Whether that Lady's gentle mind,
No longer with the form combined
Which scattered love, as stars do light,
Found sadness, where it left delight,

I dare not guess; but in this life
Of error, ignorance, and strife,
Where nothing is, but all things seem,
And we the shadows of the dream,

It is a modest creed, and yet
Pleasant if one considers it,
To own that death itself must be,
Like all the rest, a mockery.

That garden sweet, that lady fair,
And all sweet shapes and odours there,

In truth have never passed away:
'Tis we, 'tis ours, are changed; not they.

For love, and beauty, and delight,
There is no death nor change: their might
Exceeds our organs, which endure
No light, being themselves obscure.

To a Skylark

Hail to thee, blithe spirit—
    Bird thou never wert—
  That from heaven or near it
    Pourest thy full heart
In profuse strains of unpremeditated art.

  Higher still and higher
    From the earth thou springest,
  Like a cloud of fire;
    The blue deep thou wingest,
And singing still dost soar and soaring ever singest.

  In the golden lightning
    Of the sunken sun,
  O'er which clouds are brightening,
    Thou dost float and run,
Like an unbodied joy whose race is just begun.

  The pale purple even
    Melts around thy flight;
  Like a star of heaven,
    In the broad daylight
Thou art unseen, but yet I hear thy shrill delight.

  Keen as are the arrows
    Of that silver sphere
  Whose intense lamp narrows
    In the white dawn clear,
Until we hardly see, we feel that it is there.

All the earth and air
  With thy voice is loud,
As, when night is bare,
  From one lonely cloud
The moon rains out her beams, and heaven is over-
  flowed.

What thou art we know not;
  What is most like thee?
From rainbow-clouds there flow not
  Drops so bright to see
As from thy presence showers a rain of melody:—

Like a poet hidden
  In the light of thought;
Singing hymns unbidden,
  Till the world is wrought
To sympathy with hopes and fears it heeded not.

Like a high-born maiden
  In a palace-tower,
Soothing her love-laden
  Soul in secret hour
With music sweet as love, which overflows her bower:

Like a glow-worm golden
  In a dell of dew,
Scattering unbeholden
  Its aërial hue
Among the flowers and grass which screen it from the
  view:

Like a rose embowered
　In its own green leaves,
By warm winds deflowered,
　Till the scent it gives
Makes faint with too much sweet these heavy-wingéd
　thieves:

Sound of vernal showers
　On the twinkling grass,
Rain-awakened flowers—
　All that ever was
Joyous and clear and fresh—thy music doth surpass.

Teach us, sprite or bird,
　What sweet thoughts are thine:
I have never heard
　Praise of love or wine
That panted forth a flood of rapture so divine.

Chorus hymeneal
　Or triumphal chaunt,
Matched with thine, would be all
　But an empty vaunt—
A thing wherein we feel there is some hidden want.

What objects are the fountains
　Of thy happy strain?
What fields, or waves, or mountains?
　What shapes of sky or plain?
What love of thine own kind? what ignorance of pain?

With thy clear keen joyance
    Languor cannot be:
Shadow of annoyance
    Never came near thee:
Thou lovest, but ne'er knew love's sad satiety.

Waking or asleep,
    Thou of death must deem
Things more true and deep
    Than we mortals dream,
Or how could thy notes flow in such a crystal stream?

We look before and after,
    And pine for what is not:
Our sincerest laughter
    With some pain is fraught;
Our sweetest songs are those that tell of saddest
    thought.

Yet, if we could scorn
    Hate and pride and fear,
If we were things born
    Not to shed a tear,
I know not how thy joy we ever should come near.

Better than all measures
    Of delightful sound,
Better than all treasures
    That in books are found,
Thy skill to poet were, thou scorner of the ground!

Teach me half the gladness
    That thy brain must know,
Such harmonious madness
    From my lips would flow,
The world should listen then, as I am listening now!

The Cloud

I bring fresh showers for the thirsting flowers,
  From the seas and the streams;
I bear light shade for the leaves when laid
  In their noonday dreams.
From my wings are shaken the dews that waken
  The sweet buds every one,
When rocked to rest on their mother's breast,
As she dances about the sun.
  I wield the flail of the lashing hail,
And whiten the green plains under,
  And then again I dissolve it in rain,
And laugh as I pass in thunder.

I sift the snow on the mountains below,
  And their great pines groan aghast;
And all the night 'tis my pillow white,
  While I sleep in the arms of the blast.
Sublime on the towers of my skiey bowers,
  Lightning, my pilot, sits;
In a cavern under is fettered the thunder,
  It struggles and howls at fits;
Over earth and ocean, with gentle motion,
  This pilot is guiding me,
Lured by the love of the genii that move
  In the depths of the purple sea;
Over the rills, and the crags, and the hills,
  Over the lakes and the plains,
Wherever he dream, under mountain or stream,
  The Spirit he loves remains;

And I all the while bask in Heaven's blue smile,
  Whilst he is dissolving in rains.

The sanguine Sunrise, with his meteor eyes,
  And his burning plumes outspread,
Leaps on the back of my sailing rack,
  When the morning star shines dead;
As on the jag of a mountain crag,
  Which an earthquake rocks and swings,
An eagle alit one moment may sit
  In the light of its golden wings.
And when Sunset may breathe, from the lit sea beneath,
  Its ardours of rest and of love,
And the crimson pall of eve may fall
  From the depth of Heaven above,
With wings folded I rest, on mine aery nest,
  As still as a brooding dove.

That orbed maiden with white fire laden,
  Whom mortals call the Moon,
Glides glimmering o'er my fleece-like floor,
  By the midnight breezes strewn;
And wherever the beat of her unseen feet,
  Which only the angels hear,
May have broken the woof of my tent's thin roof,
  The stars peep behind her and peer;
And I laugh to see them whirl and flee,
  Like a swarm of golden bees,
When I widen the rent in my wind-built tent,
  Till the calm rivers, lakes, and seas,
Like strips of the sky fallen through me on high,
  Are each paved with the moon and these.

I bind the Sun's throne with a burning zone,
    And the Moon's with a girdle of pearl;
The volcanoes are dim, and the stars reel and swim
    When the whirlwinds my banner unfurl.
From cape to cape, with a bridge-like shape,
    Over a torrent sea,
Sunbeam-proof, I hang like a roof,—
    The mountains its columns be.
The triumphal arch through which I march
    With hurricane, fire, and snow,
When the Powers of the air are chained to my chair,
    Is the million-coloured bow;
The sphere-fire above its soft colours wove,
    While the moist Earth was laughing below.

I am the daughter of Earth and Water,
    And the nursling of the Sky;
I pass through the pores of the ocean and shores;
    I change, but I cannot die.
For after the rain when with never a stain
    The pavilion of Heaven is bare,
And the winds and sunbeams with their convex gleams
    Build up the blue dome of air,
I silently laugh at my own cenotaph,
    And out of the caverns of rain,
Like a child from the womb, like a ghost from the tomb,
    I arise and unbuild it again.

Hymn of Apollo

The sleepless Hours who watch me as I lie,
Curtained with star-inwoven tapestries
From the broad moonlight of the sky,
Fanning the busy dreams from my dim eyes,—
Waken me when their Mother, the grey Dawn,
Tells them that dreams and that the moon is gone.

Then I arise, and climbing Heaven's blue dome,
I walk over the mountains and the waves,
Leaving my robe upon the ocean foam;
My footsteps pave the clouds with fire; the caves
Are filled with my bright presence, and the air
Leaves the green earth to my embraces bare.

The sunbeams are my shafts, with which I kill
Deceit, that loves the night and fears the day;
All men who do or even imagine ill
Fly me, and from the glory of my ray
Good minds and open actions take new might,
Until diminished by the reign of night.

I feed the clouds, the rainbows, and the flowers
With their ethereal colours; the Moon's globe
And the pure stars in their eternal bowers
Are tinctured with my power as with a robe;
Whatever lamps on Earth or Heaven may shine
Are portions of one power, which is mine.

I stand at noon upon the peak of Heaven,
Then with unwilling steps I wander down

Into the clouds of the Atlantic even;
For grief that I depart they weep and frown;
What look is more delightful than the smile
With which I soothe them from the western isle?

I am the eye with which the Universe
Beholds itself and knows itself divine;
All harmony of instrument or verse,
All prophecy, all medicine are mine.
All light of Art or Nature;—to my song
Victory and praise in their own right belong.

Song of Proserpine

Sacred Goddess, Mother Earth,
Thou from whose immortal bosom
Gods and men and beasts have birth,
Leaf and blade, and bud and blossom,
Breathe thine influence most divine
On thine own child, Proserpine.

If with mists of evening dew
Thou dost nourish these young flowers
Till they grow in scent and hue
Fairest children of the Hours,
Breathe thine influence most divine
On thine own child, Proserpine.

Arethusa

Arethusa arose
From her couch of snows
In the Acroceraunian mountains,—
From cloud and from crag,
With many a jag,
Shepherding her bright fountains.
She leapt down the rocks,
With her rainbow locks
Streaming among the streams;—
Her steps paved with green
The downward ravine
Which slopes to the western gleams;
And gliding and springing
She went, ever singing,
In murmurs as soft as sleep;
The Earth seemed to love her,
And Heaven smiled above her,
As she lingered towards the deep.

Then Alpheus bold,
On his glacier cold,
With his trident the mountains strook;
And opened a chasm
In the rocks—with the spasm
All Erymanthus shook.
And the black south wind
It unsealed behind
The urns of the silent snow,
And earthquake and thunder
Did rend in sunder

The bars of the springs below.
And the beard and the hair
Of the River-god were
Seen through the torrent's sweep,
As he followed the light
Of the fleet nymph's flight
To the brink of the Dorian deep.

'Oh, save me! Oh, guide me!
And bid the deep hide me,
For he grasps me now by the hair!'
The loud Ocean heard,
To its blue depth stirred,
And divided at her prayer;
And under the water
The Earth's white daughter
Fled like a sunny beam;
Behind her descended
Her billows, unblended
With the brackish Dorian stream:—
Like a gloomy stain
On the emerald main
Alpheus rushed behind,—
As an eagle pursuing
A dove to its ruin
Down the streams of the cloudy wind.

Under the bowers
Where the Ocean Powers
Sit on their pearled thrones;
Through the coral woods
Of the weltering floods,

Over heaps of unvalued stones;
Through the dim beams
Which amid the streams
Weave a network of coloured light;
And under the caves,
Where the shadowy waves
Are as green as the forest's night:—
Outspeeding the shark,
And the sword-fish dark,
Under the Ocean's foam,
And up through the rifts
Of the mountain clifts
They passed to their Dorian home.

And now from their fountains
In Enna's mountains,
Down one vale where the morning basks,
Like friends once parted
Grown single-hearted,
They ply their watery tasks.
At sunrise they leap
From their cradles steep
In the cave of the shelving hill;
At noontide they flow
Through the woods below
And the meadows of asphodel;
And at night they sleep
In the rocking deep
Beneath the Ortygian shore;—
Like spirits that lie
In the azure sky
When they love but live no more.

Song

Rarely, rarely, comest thou,
Spirit of Delight!
Wherefore hast thou left me now
Many a day and night?
Many a weary night and day
'Tis since thou art fled away.

How shall ever one like me
Win thee back again?
With the joyous and the free
Thou wilt scoff at pain.
Spirit false! thou hast forgot
All but those who need thee not.

As a lizard with the shade
Of a trembling leaf,
Thou with sorrow art dismayed;
Even the sighs of grief
Reproach thee, that thou art not near,
And reproach thou wilt not hear.

Let me set my mournful ditty
To a merry measure;
Thou wilt never come for pity,
Thou wilt come for pleasure;
Pity then will cut away
Those cruel wings, and thou wilt stay.

I love all that thou lovest,
Spirit of Delight!

The fresh Earth in new leaves dressed,
And the starry night;
Autumn evening, and the morn
When the golden mists are born.

I love snow, and all the forms
Of the radiant frost;
I love waves, and winds, and storms,
Everything almost
Which is Nature's, and may be
Untainted by man's misery.

I love tranquil solitude,
And such society
As is quiet, wise, and good
Between thee and me
What difference? but thou dost possess
The things I seek, not love them less.

I love Love—though he has wings,
And like light can flee,
But above all other things,
Spirit, I love thee—
Thou art love and life! Oh, come,
Make once more my heart thy home.

Adonais

I weep for Adonais—he is dead!
O, weep for Adonais! though our tears
Thaw not the frost which binds so dear a head!
And thou, sad Hour, selected from all years
To mourn our loss, rouse thy obscure compeers,
And teach them thine own sorrow, say: 'With me
Died Adonais; till the Future dares
Forget the Past, his fate and fame shall be
An echo and a light unto eternity!'

Where wert thou, mighty Mother, when he lay,
When thy Son lay, pierced by the shaft which flies
In darkness? where was lorn Urania
When Adonais died? With veiled eyes,
Mid listening Echoes, in her Paradise
She sate, while one, with soft enamoured breath,
Rekindled all the fading melodies
With which, like flowers that mock the corse beneath,
He had adorned and hid the coming bulk of death.

O, weep for Adonais—he is dead!
Wake, melancholy Mother, wake and weep!
Yet wherefore? Quench within their burning bed
Thy fiery tears, and let thy loud heart keep
Like his, a mute and uncomplaining sleep;
For he is gone, where all things wise and fair
Descend;—oh, dream not that the amorous Deep
Will yet restore him to the vital air;
Death feeds on his mute voice, and laughs at our despair.

Most musical of mourners, weep again!
Lament anew, Urania!—He died,
Who was the Sire of an immortal strain,
Blind, old, and lonely, when his country's pride,
The priest, the slave, and the liberticide
Trampled and mocked with many a loathed rite
Of lust and blood; he went, unterrified,
Into the gulf of death; but his clear Sprite
Yet reigns o'er earth; the third among the sons of light.

Most musical of mourners, weep anew!
Not all to that bright station dared to climb;
And happier they their happiness who knew,
Whose tapers yet burn through that night of time
In which suns perished; others more sublime,
Struck by the envious wrath of man or god,
Have sunk, extinct in their refulgent prime;
And some yet live, treading the thorny road
Which leads, through toil and hate, to Fame's serene
    abode.

But now, thy youngest, dearest one, has perished—
The nursling of thy widowhood, who grew,
Like a pale flower by some sad maiden cherished,
And fed with true-love tears, instead of dew;
Most musical of mourners, weep anew!
Thy extreme hope, the loveliest and the last,
The bloom, whose petals nipped before they blew
Died on the promise of the fruit, is waste;
The broken lily lies—the storm is overpast.

To that high Capital, where kingly Death
Keeps his pale court in beauty and decay,
He came; and bought, with price of purest breath,
A grave among the eternal.—Come away!
Haste, while the vault of blue Italian day
Is yet his fitting charnel-roof! while still
He lies, as if in dewy sleep he lay;
Awake him not! surely he takes his fill
Of deep and liquid rest, forgetful of all ill.

He will awake no more, oh, never more!—
Within the twilight chamber spreads apace
The shadow of white Death, and at the door
Invisible Corruption waits to trace
His extreme way to her dim dwelling-place;
The eternal Hunger sits, but pity and awe
Soothe her pale rage, nor dares she to deface
So fair a prey, till darkness, and the law
Of change, shall o'er his sleep the mortal curtain draw.

O, weep for Adonais!—The quick Dreams,
The passion-winged Ministers of thought,
Who were his flocks, whom near the living streams
Of his young spirit he fed, and whom he taught
The love which was its music, wander not,—
Wander no more, from kindling brain to brain,
But droop there, whence they sprung; and mourn their lot
Round the cold heart, where, after their sweet pain,
They ne'er will gather strength, or find a home again.

And one with trembling hands clasps his cold head,
And fans him with her moonlight wings, and cries,

'Our love, our hope, our sorrow, is not dead;
See, on the silken fringe of his faint eyes,
Like dew upon a sleeping flower, there lies
A tear some Dream has loosened from his brain.'
Lost Angel of a ruined Paradise!
She knew not 'twas her own; as with no stain
She faded, like a cloud which had outwept its rain.

One from a lucid urn of starry dew
Washed his light limbs as if embalming them;
Another clipped her profuse locks, and threw
The wreath upon him, like an anadem,
Which frozen tears instead of pearls begem;
Another in her wilful grief would break
Her bow and winged reeds, as if to stem
A greater loss with one which was more weak;
And dull the barbed fire against his frozen cheek.

Another Splendour on his mouth alit,
That mouth, whence it was wont to draw the breath
Which gave it strength to pierce the guarded wit,
And pass into the panting heart beneath
With lightning and with music: the damp death
Quenched its caress upon his icy lips;
And, as a dying meteor stains a wreath
Of moonlight vapour, which the cold night clips,
It flushed through his pale limbs, and passed to its
  eclipse.

And others came... Desires and Adorations,
Winged Persuasions and veiled Destinies,
Splendours, and Glooms, and glimmering Incarnations

Of hopes and fears, and twilight Phantasies;
And Sorrow, with her family of Sighs,
And Pleasure, blind with tears, led by the gleam
Of her own dying smile instead of eyes,
Came in slow pomp;—the moving pomp might seem
Like pageantry of mist on an autumnal stream.

All he had loved, and moulded into thought,
From shape, and hue, and odour, and sweet sound,
Lamented Adonais. Morning sought
Her eastern watch-tower, and her hair unbound,
Wet with the tears which should adorn the ground,
Dimm'd the aëreal eyes that kindle day;
Afar the melancholy thunder moaned,
Pale Ocean in unquiet slumber lay,
And the wild Winds flew round, sobbing in their dismay.

Lost Echo sits amid the voiceless mountains,
And feeds her grief with his remembered lay,
And will no more reply to winds or fountains,
Or amorous birds perched on the young green spray,
Or herdsman's horn, or bell at closing day;
Since she can mimic not his lips, more dear
Than those for whose disdain she pined away
Into a shadow of all sounds:—a drear
Murmur, between their songs, is all the woodmen hear.

Grief made the young Spring wild, and she threw down
Her kindling buds, as if she Autumn were,
Or they dead leaves; since her delight is flown,
For whom should she have waked the sullen year?
To Phoebus was not Hyacinth so dear

Nor to himself Narcissus, as to both
Thou, Adonais: wan they stand and sere
Amid the faint companions of their youth,
With dew all turned to tears; odour, to sighing ruth.

Thy spirit's sister, the lorn nightingale
Mourns not her mate with such melodious pain;
Not so the eagle, who like thee could scale
Heaven, and could nourish in the sun's domain
Her mighty youth with morning, doth complain,
Soaring and screaming round her empty nest,
As Albion wails for thee: the curse of Cain
Light on his head who pierced thy innocent breast,
And scared the angel soul that was its earthly guest!

Ah, woe is me! Winter is come and gone,
But grief returns with the revolving year;
The airs and streams renew their joyous tone;
The ants, the bees, the swallows reappear;
Fresh leaves and flowers deck the dead Season's bier;
The amorous birds now pair in every brake,
And build their mossy homes in field and brere;
And the green lizard, and the golden snake,
Like unimprisoned flames, out of their trance awake.

Through wood and stream and field and hill and Ocean
A quickening life from the Earth's heart has burst
As it has ever done, with change and motion,
From the great morning of the world when first
God dawned on Chaos; in its stream immersed,
The lamps of Heaven flash with a softer light;

All baser things pant with life's sacred thirst;
Diffuse themselves; and spend in love's delight
The beauty and the joy of their renewed might.

The leprous corpse, touched by this spirit tender,
Exhales itself in flowers of gentle breath;
Like incarnations of the stars, when splendour
Is changed to fragrance, they illumine death
And mock the merry worm that wakes beneath;
Nought we know, dies. Shall that alone which knows
Be as a sword consumed before the sheath
By sightless lightning?—the intense atom glows
A moment, then is quenched in a most cold repose.

Alas! that all we loved of him should be,
But for our grief, as if it had not been,
And grief itself be mortal! Woe is me!
Whence are we, and why are we? of what scene
The actors or spectators? Great and mean
Meet massed in death, who lends what life must borrow.
As long as skies are blue, and fields are green,
Evening must usher night, night urge the morrow,
Month follow month with woe, and year wake year to
    sorrow.

He will awake no more, oh, never more!
'Wake thou,' cried Misery, 'childless Mother, rise
Out of thy sleep, and slake, in thy heart's core,
A wound more fierce than his with tears and sighs.'
And all the Dreams that watched Urania's eyes,
And all the Echoes whom their sister's song

Had held in holy silence, cried: 'Arise!'
Swift as a Thought by the snake Memory stung,
From her ambrosial rest the fading Splendour sprung.

She rose like an autumnal Night, that springs
Out of the East, and follows wild and drear
The golden Day, which, on eternal wings,
Even as a ghost abandoning a bier,
Had left the Earth a corpse. Sorrow and fear
So struck, so roused, so rapt Urania;
So saddened round her like an atmosphere
Of stormy mist; so swept her on her way
Even to the mournful place where Adonais lay.

Out of her secret Paradise she sped,
Through camps and cities rough with stone, and steel,
And human hearts, which to her aery tread
Yielding not, wounded the invisible
Palms of her tender feet where'er they fell:
And barbed tongues, and thoughts more sharp than they,
Rent the soft Form they never could repel,
Whose sacred blood, like the young tears of May,
Paved with eternal flowers that undeserving way.

In the death-chamber for a moment Death,
Shamed by the presence of that living Might,
Blushed to annihilation, and the breath
Revisited those lips, and Life's pale light
Flashed through those limbs, so late her dear delight.
'Leave me not wild and drear and comfortless,
As silent lightning leaves the starless night!

Leave me not!' cried Urania: her distress
Roused Death: Death rose and smiled, and met her vain
  caress.

'Stay yet awhile! speak to me once again;
Kiss me, so long but as a kiss may live;
And in my heartless breast and burning brain
That word, that kiss, shall all thoughts else survive,
With food of saddest memory kept alive,
Now thou art dead, as if it were a part
Of thee, my Adonais! I would give
All that I am to be as thou now art!
But I am chained to Time, and cannot thence depart!

'O gentle child, beautiful as thou wert,
Why didst thou leave the trodden paths of men
Too soon, and with weak hands though mighty heart
Dare the unpastured dragon in his den?
Defenceless as thou wert, oh, where was then
Wisdom the mirrored shield, or scorn the spear?
Or hadst thou waited the full cycle, when
Thy spirit should have filled its crescent sphere,
The monsters of life's waste had fled from thee like deer.

'The herded wolves, bold only to pursue;
The obscene ravens, clamorous o'er the dead;
The vultures to the conqueror's banner true
Who feed where Desolation first has fed,
And whose wings rain contagion;—how they fled,
When, like Apollo, from his golden bow
The Pythian of the age one arrow sped

And smiled!—The spoilers tempt no second blow,
They fawn on the proud feet that spurn them lying low.

'The sun comes forth, and many reptiles spawn;
He sets, and each ephemeral insect then
Is gathered into death without a dawn,
And the immortal stars awake again;
So is it in the world of living men:
A godlike mind soars forth, in its delight
Making earth bare and veiling heaven, and when
It sinks, the swarms that dimmed or shared its light
Leave to its kindred lamps the spirit's awful night.'

Thus ceased she: and the mountain shepherds came,
Their garlands sere, their magic mantles rent;
The Pilgrim of Eternity, whose fame
Over his living head like Heaven is bent,
An early but enduring monument,
Came, veiling all the lightnings of his song
In sorrow; from her wilds Ierne sent
The sweetest lyrist of her saddest wrong,
And Love taught Grief to fall like music from his tongue.

Midst others of less note, came one frail Form,
A phantom among men; companionless
As the last cloud of an expiring storm
Whose thunder is its knell; he, as I guess,
Had gazed on Nature's naked loveliness,
Actaeon-like, and now he fled astray
With feeble steps o'er the world's wilderness,
And his own thoughts, along that rugged way,
Pursued, like raging hounds, their father and their prey.

A pardlike Spirit beautiful and swift—
A Love in desolation masked;—a Power
Girt round with weakness;—it can scarce uplift
The weight of the superincumbent hour;
It is a dying lamp, a falling shower,
A breaking billow;—even whilst we speak
Is it not broken? On the withering flower
The killing sun smiles brightly: on a cheek
The life can burn in blood, even while the heart may
    break.

His head was bound with pansies overblown,
And faded violets, white, and pied, and blue;
And a light spear topped with a cypress cone,
Round whose rude shaft dark ivy-tresses grew
Yet dripping with the forest's noonday dew,
Vibrated, as the ever-beating heart
Shook the weak hand that grasped it; of that crew
He came the last, neglected and apart;
A herd-abandoned deer struck by the hunter's dart.

All stood aloof, and at his partial moan
Smiled through their tears; well knew that gentle band
Who in another's fate now wept his own,
As in the accents of an unknown land
He sung new sorrow; sad Urania scanned
The Stranger's mien, and murmured: 'Who art thou?'
He answered not, but with a sudden hand
Made bare his branded and ensanguined brow,
Which was like Cain's or Christ's—oh! that it should be
    so!

What softer voice is hushed over the dead?
Athwart what brow is that dark mantle thrown?
What form leans sadly o'er the white death-bed,
In mockery of monumental stone,
The heavy heart heaving without a moan?
If it be He, who, gentlest of the wise,
Taught, soothed, loved, honoured the departed one,
Let me not vex, with inharmonious sighs,
The silence of that heart's accepted sacrifice.

Our Adonais has drunk poison—oh!
What deaf and viperous murderer could crown
Life's early cup with such a draught of woe?
The nameless worm would now itself disown:
It felt, yet could escape, the magic tone
Whose prelude held all envy, hate, and wrong,
But what was howling in one breast alone,
Silent with expectation of the song,
Whose master's hand is cold, whose silver lyre unstrung.

Live thou, whose infamy is not thy fame!
Live! fear no heavier chastisement from me,
Thou noteless blot on a remembered name!
But be thyself, and know thyself to be!
And ever at thy season be thou free
To spill the venom when thy fangs o'erflow:
Remorse and Self-contempt shall cling to thee;
Hot Shame shall burn upon thy secret brow,
And like a beaten hound tremble thou shalt—as now.

Nor let us weep that our delight is fled
Far from these carrion kites that scream below;

He wakes or sleeps with the enduring dead;
Thou canst not soar where he is sitting now –
Dust to the dust! but the pure spirit shall flow
Back to the burning fountain whence it came,
A portion of the Eternal, which must glow
Through time and change, unquenchably the same,
Whilst thy cold embers choke the sordid hearth of shame.

Peace, peace! he is not dead, he doth not sleep—
He hath awakened from the dream of life—
'Tis we, who lost in stormy visions, keep
With phantoms an unprofitable strife,
And in mad trance, strike with our spirit's knife
Invulnerable nothings.—We decay
Like corpses in a charnel; fear and grief
Convulse us and consume us day by day,
And cold hopes swarm like worms within our living clay.

He has outsoared the shadow of our night;
Envy and calumny and hate and pain,
And that unrest which men miscall delight,
Can touch him not and torture not again;
From the contagion of the world's slow stain
He is secure, and now can never mourn
A heart grown cold, a head grown grey in vain;
Nor, when the spirit's self has ceased to burn,
With sparkless ashes load an unlamented urn.

He lives, he wakes—'tis Death is dead, not he;
Mourn not for Adonais.—Thou young Dawn,
Turn all thy dew to splendour, for from thee
The spirit thou lamentest is not gone;

Ye caverns and ye forests, cease to moan!
Cease, ye faint flowers and fountains, and thou Air
Which like a mourning veil thy scarf hadst thrown
O'er the abandoned Earth, now leave it bare
Even to the joyous stars which smile on its despair!

He is made one with Nature: there is heard
His voice in all her music, from the moan
Of thunder, to the song of night's sweet bird;
He is a presence to be felt and known
In darkness and in light, from herb and stone,
Spreading itself where'er that Power may move
Which has withdrawn his being to its own;
Which wields the world with never-wearied love,
Sustains it from beneath, and kindles it above.

He is a portion of the loveliness
Which once he made more lovely: he doth bear
His part, while the one Spirit's plastic stress
Sweeps through the dull dense world, compelling there
All new successions to the forms they wear;
Torturing th' unwilling dross that checks its flight
To its own likeness, as each mass may bear;
And bursting in its beauty and its might
From trees and beasts and men into the
  Heavens' light.

The splendours of the firmament of time
May be eclipsed, but are extinguished not;
Like stars to their appointed height they climb,
And death is a low mist which cannot blot
The brightness it may veil. When lofty thought

Lifts a young heart above its mortal lair,
And love and life contend in it, for what
Shall be its earthly doom, the dead live there
And move like winds of light on dark and stormy air.

The inheritors of unfulfilled renown
Rose from their thrones, built beyond mortal thought,
Far in the Unapparent. Chatterton
Rose pale,—his solemn agony had not
Yet faded from him; Sidney, as he fought
And as he fell and as he lived and loved
Sublimely mild, a Spirit without spot,
Arose; and Lucan, by his death approved:
Oblivion as they rose shrank like a thing reproved.

And many more, whose names on Earth are dark,
But whose transmitted effluence cannot die
So long as fire outlives the parent spark,
Rose, robed in dazzling immortality.
'Thou art become as one of us,' they cry,
'It was for thee yon kingless sphere has long
Swung blind in unascended majesty,
Silent alone amid an Heaven of Song.
Assume thy winged throne, thou Vesper of our throng!'

Who mourns for Adonais? Oh, come forth,
Fond wretch! and know thyself and him aright.
Clasp with thy panting soul the pendulous Earth;
As from a centre, dart thy spirit's light
Beyond all worlds, until its spacious might
Satiate the void circumference: then shrink
Even to a point within our day and night;

And keep thy heart light lest it make thee sink
When hope has kindled hope, and lured thee to the
 brink.

Or go to Rome, which is the sepulchre,
Oh, not of him, but of our joy: 'tis nought
That ages, empires, and religions there
Lie buried in the ravage they have wrought;
For such as he can lend,—they borrow not
Glory from those who made the world their prey;
And he is gathered to the kings of thought
Who waged contention with their time's decay,
And of the past are all that cannot pass away.

Go thou to Rome,—at once the Paradise,
The grave, the city, and the wilderness;
And where its wrecks like shattered mountains rise,
And flowering weeds, and fragrant copses dress
The bones of Desolation's nakedness
Pass, till the spirit of the spot shall lead
Thy footsteps to a slope of green access
Where, like an infant's smile, over the dead
A light of laughing flowers along the grass
 is spread;

And grey walls moulder round, on which dull Time
Feeds, like slow fire upon a hoary brand;
And one keen pyramid with wedge sublime,
Pavilioning the dust of him who planned
This refuge for his memory, doth stand
Like flame transformed to marble; and beneath,
A field is spread, on which a newer band

Have pitched in Heaven's smile their camp of death,
Welcoming him we lose with scarce extinguished breath.

Here pause: these graves are all too young as yet
To have outgrown the sorrow which consigned
Its charge to each; and if the seal is set,
Here, on one fountain of a mourning mind,
Break it not thou! too surely shalt thou find
Thine own well full, if thou returnest home,
Of tears and gall. From the world's bitter wind
Seek shelter in the shadow of the tomb.
What Adonais is, why fear we to become?

The One remains, the many change and pass;
Heaven's light forever shines, Earth's shadows fly;
Life, like a dome of many-coloured glass,
Stains the white radiance of Eternity,
Until Death tramples it to fragments.—Die,
If thou wouldst be with that which thou dost seek!
Follow where all is fled!—Rome's azure sky,
Flowers, ruins, statues, music, words, are weak
The glory they transfuse with fitting truth to speak.

Why linger, why turn back, why shrink, my Heart?
Thy hopes are gone before: from all things here
They have departed; thou shouldst now depart!
A light is passed from the revolving year,
And man, and woman; and what still is dear
Attracts to crush, repels to make thee wither.
The soft sky smiles,—the low wind whispers near:
'Tis Adonais calls! oh, hasten thither,
No more let Life divide what Death can join together.

That Light whose smile kindles the Universe,
That Beauty in which all things work and move,
That Benediction which the eclipsing Curse
Of birth can quench not, that sustaining Love
Which through the web of being blindly wove
By man and beast and earth and air and sea,
Burns bright or dim, as each are mirrors of
The fire for which all thirst, now beams on me,
Consuming the last clouds of cold mortality.

The breath whose might I have invoked in song
Descends on me; my spirit's bark is driven
Far from the shore, far from the trembling throng
Whose sails were never to the tempest given;
The massy earth and sphered skies are riven!
I am borne darkly, fearfully, afar;
Whilst, burning through the inmost veil of Heaven,
The soul of Adonais, like a star,
Beacons from the abode where the Eternal are.

The Fugitives

I

The waters are flashing,
The white hail is dashing,
The lightnings are glancing,
The hoar-spray is dancing—
Away!

The whirlwind is rolling,
The thunder is tolling,
The forest is swinging,
The minster bells ringing—
Come away!

The Earth is like Ocean,
Wreck-strewn and in motion:
Bird, beast, man and worm
Have crept out of the storm—
Come away!

II

'Our boat has one sail
And the helmsman is pale;—
A bold pilot I trow,
Who should follow us now,'—
Shouted he—

And she cried: 'Ply the oar!
Put off gaily from shore!'—
As she spoke, bolts of death
Mixed with hail, specked their path
O'er the sea.

And from isle, tower and rock,
The blue beacon-cloud broke,
And though dumb in the blast,
The red cannon flashed fast
From the lee.

III

And 'Fear'st thou?' and 'Fear'st thou?'
And Seest thou?' and 'Hear'st thou?'
And 'Drive we not free
O'er the terrible sea,
I and thou?'

One boat-cloak did cover
The loved and the lover—
Their blood beats one measure,
They murmur proud pleasure
Soft and low;—

While around the lashed Ocean,
Like mountains in motion,
Is withdrawn and uplifted,
Sunk, shattered and shifted
To and fro.

IV

In the court of the fortress
Beside the pale portress,
Like a bloodhound well beaten
The bridegroom stands, eaten
By shame;

On the topmost watch-turret,
As a death-boding spirit
Stands the gray tyrant father,
To his voice the mad weather
Seems tame;

And with curses as wild
As e'er clung to child,
He devotes to the blast,
The best, loveliest and last
Of his name!

To — (When passion's trance is overpast)

When passion's trance is overpast,
If tenderness and truth could last,
Or live, whilst all wild feelings keep
Some mortal slumber, dark and deep,
I should not weep, I should not weep!

It were enough to feel, to see,
Thy soft eyes gazing tenderly,
And dream the rest—and burn and be
The secret food of fires unseen,
Couldst thou but be as thou hast been,

After the slumber of the year
The woodland violets reappear;
All things revive in field or grove,
And sky and sea, but two, which move
And form all others, life and love.

To — (One word is too often profaned)

One word is too often profaned
For me to profane it,
One feeling too falsely disdained
For thee to disdain it;
One hope is too like despair
For prudence to smother,
And pity from thee more dear
Than that from another.

I can give not what men call love,
But wilt thou accept not
The worship the heart lifts above
And the Heavens reject not,—
The desire of the moth for the star,
Of the night for the morrow,
The devotion to something afar
From the sphere of our sorrow?

The cold earth swept below

The cold earth slept below;
    Above the cold sky shone;
        And all around,
        With a chilling sound,
From caves of ice and fields of snow
The breath of night like death did flow
        Beneath the sinking moon.

The wintry hedge was black;
    The green grass was not seen;
        The birds did rest
        On the bare thorn's breast,
Whose roots, beside the pathway track,
Had bound their folds o'er many a crack
        Which the frost had made between.

Thine eyes glow'd in the glare
    Of the moon's dying light;
        As a fen-fire's beam
        On a sluggish stream
Gleams dimly—so the moon shone there,
And it yellow'd the strings of thy tangled hair,
        That shook in the wind of night.

The moon made thy lips pale, beloved;
    The wind made thy bosom chill;
        The night did shed
        On thy dear head

Its frozen dew, and thou didst lie
Where the bitter breath of the naked sky
   Might visit thee at will.

When the Lamp is Shattered

When the lamp is shattered
The light in dust lies dead –
  When the cloud is scattered
The rainbow's glory is shed.
  When the lute is broken,
Sweet tones are remembered not;
  When the lips have spoken,
Loved accents are soon forgot.

  As music and splendour
Survive not the lamp and the lute,
  The heart's echoes render
No song when the spirit is mute: –
  No song but sad dirges,
Like the wind through a ruined cell,
  Or the mournful surges
That ring the dead seaman's knell.

  When hearts have once mingled
Love first leaves the well-built nest
  The weak one is singled
To endure what it once possessed.
  O Love! who bewailest
The frailty of all things here,
  Why choose you the frailest
For your cradle, your home, and your bier?

  Its passions rock thee
As the storms rock the ravens on high;
  Bright reason will mock thee,

Like the sun from a wintry sky.
   From thy nest every rafter
Will rot, and thine eagle home
   Leave thee naked to laughter,
When leaves fall and cold winds come.

Lines written in the Bay of Lerici

She left me at the silent time
When the moon had ceased to climb
The azure path of Heaven's steep,
And like an albatross asleep,
Balanced on her wings of light,
Hovered in the purple night,
Ere she sought her ocean nest
In the chambers of the West.
She left me, and I stayed alone
Thinking over every tone
Which, though silent to the ear,
The enchanted heart could hear,
Like notes which die when born, but still
Haunt the echoes of the hill;
And feeling ever—oh, too much!—
The soft vibration of her touch,
As if her gentle hand, even now,
Lightly trembled on my brow;
And thus, although she absent were,
Memory gave me all of her
That even Fancy dares to claim:—
Her presence had made weak and tame
All passions, and I lived alone
In the time which is our own;
The past and future were forgot,
As they had been, and would be, not.
But soon, the guardian angel gone,
The daemon reassumed his throne
In my faint heart. I dare not speak
My thoughts, but thus disturbed and weak

I sat and saw the vessels glide
Over the ocean bright and wide,
Like spirit-winged chariots sent
O'er some serenest element
For ministrations strange and far;
As if to some Elysian star
Sailed for drink to medicine
Such sweet and bitter pain as mine.
And the wind that winged their flight
From the land came fresh and light,
And the scent of winged flowers,
And the coolness of the hours
Of dew, and sweet warmth left by day,
Were scattered o'er the twinkling bay.
And the fisher with his lamp
And spear about the low rocks damp
Crept, and struck the fish which came
To worship the delusive flame.
Too happy they, whose pleasure sought
Extinguishes all sense and thought
Of the regret that pleasure leaves,
Destroying life alone, not peace!

The Zucca

Summer was dead and Autumn was expiring,
And infant Winter laughed upon the land
All cloudlessly and cold;—when I, desiring
More in this world than any understand,
Wept o'er the beauty, which like sea retiring,
Had left the earth bare as the wave-worn sand
Of my poor heart, and o'er the grass and flowers
Pale for the falsehood of the flattering hours.

Summer was dead, but I yet lived to weep
The instability of all but weeping;
And on the earth lulled in her winter sleep
I woke, and envied her as she was sleeping.
Too happy Earth! over thy face shall creep
The wakening vernal airs, until thou, leaping
From unremembered dreams, shalt ... see
No death divide thy immortality.

I loved—O no, I mean not one of ye,
Or any earthly one, though ye are dear
As human heart to human heart may be;—
I loved, I know not what—but this low sphere
And all that it contains, contains not thee,
Thou, whom seen no where, I feel everywhere,
Dim object of my soul's idolatry.
Veiled art thou like ... a star.

By Heaven and Earth, from all whose shapes thou flowest,
Neither to be contained, delayed, or hidden,
Making divine the loftiest and the lowest,

When for a moment thou art not forbidden
To live within the life which thou bestowest;
And leaving noblest things vacant and chidden,
Cold as a corpse after the spirit's flight,
Blank as the sun after the birth of night.

In winds, and trees, and streams, and all things common,
In music and the sweet unconscious tone
Of animals, and voices which are human,
Meant to express some feelings of their own;
In the soft motions and rare smile of woman,
In flowers and leaves, and in the fresh grass shewn,
Or dying in the autumn, I the most
Adore thee present or lament thee lost.

And thus I went, lamenting when I saw
A plant upon the river's margin lie,
Like one who loved beyond his Nature's law,
And in despair had cast him down to die;
Its leaves which had outlived the frost, the thaw
Had blighted as a heart which hatred's eye
Can blast not, but which pity kills; the dew
Lay on its spotted leaves like tears too true.

The Heavens had wept upon it, but the Earth
Had crushed it on her unmaternal breast.

I bore it to my chamber, and I planted
It in a vase full of the lightest mould;
The winter beams which out of Heaven slanted
Fell through the window panes, disrobed of cold,
Upon its leaves and flowers; the star which panted

In evening for the Day, whose car has rolled
Over the horizon's wave, with looks of light
Smiled on it from the threshold of the night.

The mitigated influences of air
And light revived the plant, and from it grew
Strong leaves and tendrils, and its flowers fair,
Full as a cup with the vine's burning dew,
O'erflowed with golden colours; an atmosphere
Of vital warmth infolded it anew,
And every impulse sent to every part
The unbeheld pulsations of its heart.

Well might the plant grow beautiful and strong,
Even if the sun and air had smiled not on it;
For one wept o'er it all the winter long
Tears pure as Heaven's rain, which fell upon it
Hour after hour; for sounds of softest song
Mixed with the stringed melodies that won it
To leave the gentle lips on which it slept,
Had loosed the heart of him who sat and wept.

Had loosed his heart, and shook the leaves and flowers
On which he wept, the while the savage storm
Waked by the darkest of December's hours
Was raving round the chamber hushed and warm;
The birds were shivering in their leafless bowers,
The fish were frozen in the pools, the form
Of every summer plant was dead
Whilst this ...

To Jane: The Invitation

Best and brightest, come away!
Fairer far than this fair Day,
Which, like thee to those in sorrow,
Comes to bid a sweet good-morrow
To the rough Year just awake

In its cradle on the brake.
The brightest hour of unborn Spring,
Through the winter wandering,
Found, it seems, the halcyon Morn
To hoar February born,

Bending from Heaven, in azure mirth,
It kissed the forehead of the Earth,
And smiled upon the silent sea,
And bade the frozen streams be free,
And waked to music all their fountains,

And breathed upon the frozen mountains,
And like a prophetess of May
Strewed flowers upon the barren way,
Making the wintry world appear
Like one on whom thou smilest, dear.

Away, away, from men and towns,
To the wild wood and the downs—
To the silent wilderness
Where the soul need not repress
Its music lest it should not find

An echo in another's mind,
While the touch of Nature's art
Harmonizes heart to heart.
I leave this notice on my door
For each accustomed visitor:—

'I am gone into the fields
To take what this sweet hour yields;—
Reflection, you may come to-morrow,
Sit by the fireside with Sorrow.—
You with the unpaid bill, Despair,—
You, tiresome verse-reciter, Care,—

'I will pay you in the grave,—
Death will listen to your stave.
Expectation too, be off!
To-day is for itself enough;

'Hope, in pity mock not Woe
With smiles, nor follow where I go;
Long having lived on thy sweet food,
At length I find one moment's good
After long pain—with all your love,
This you never told me of.'

Radiant Sister of the Day,
Awake! arise! and come away!
To the wild woods and the plains,
And the pools where winter rains

Image all their roof of leaves,
Where the pine its garland weaves

Of sapless green and ivy dun
Round stems that never kiss the sun;
Where the lawns and pastures be,

And the sandhills of the sea;—
Where the melting hoar-frost wets
The daisy-star that never sets,
And wind-flowers, and violets,
Which yet join not scent to hue,

Crown the pale year weak and new;
When the night is left behind
In the deep east, dun and blind,
And the blue noon is over us,
And the multitudinous

Billows murmur at our feet,
Where the earth and ocean meet,
And all things seem only one
In the universal sun.

To Jane: The Recollection

Now the last day of many days,
All beautiful and bright as thou,
The loveliest and the last, is dead,
Rise, Memory, and write its praise!
Up,—to thy wonted work! come, trace
The epitaph of glory fled,—
For now the Earth has changed its face,
A frown is on the Heaven's brow.

We wandered to the Pine Forest
That skirts the Ocean's foam,
The lightest wind was in its nest,
The tempest in its home.
The whispering waves were half asleep,
The clouds were gone to play,
And on the bosom of the deep
The smile of Heaven lay;
It seemed as if the hour were one
Sent from beyond the skies,
Which scattered from above the sun
A light of Paradise.

We paused amid the pines that stood
The giants of the waste,
Tortured by storms to shapes as rude
As serpents interlaced;
And, soothed by every azure breath,
That under Heaven is blown,
To harmonies and hues beneath,
As tender as its own,

Now all the tree-tops lay asleep,
Like green waves on the sea,
As still as in the silent deep
The ocean woods may be.

How calm it was!—the silence there
By such a chain was bound
That even the busy woodpecker
Made stiller by her sound
The inviolable quietness;
The breath of peace we drew
With its soft motion made not less
The calm that round us grew.
There seemed from the remotest seat
Of the white mountain waste,
To the soft flower beneath our feet,
A magic circle traced,—
A spirit interfused around
A thrilling, silent life,—
To momentary peace it bound
Our mortal nature's strife;
And still I felt the centre of
The magic circle there
Was one fair form that filled with love
The lifeless atmosphere.

We paused beside the pools that lie
Under the forest bough,—
Each seemed as 'twere a little sky
Gulfed in a world below;
A firmament of purple light
Which in the dark earth lay,

More boundless than the depth of night,
And purer than the day—
In which the lovely forests grew,
As in the upper air,
More perfect both in shape and hue
Than any spreading there.
There lay the glade and neighbouring lawn,
And through the dark green wood
The white sun twinkling like the dawn
Out of a speckled cloud.
Sweet views which in our world above
Can never well be seen,
Were imaged by the water's love
Of that fair forest green.
And all was interfused beneath
With an Elysian glow,
An atmosphere without a breath,
A softer day below.
Like one beloved the scene had lent
To the dark water's breast,
Its every leaf and lineament
With more than truth expressed;
Until an envious wind crept by,
Like an unwelcome thought,
Which from the mind's too faithful eye
Blots one dear image out.
Though thou art ever fair and kind,
The forests ever green,
Less oft is peace in Shelley's mind,
Than calm in waters, seen.

The Magnetic Lady to Her Patient

'Sleep, sleep on! forget thy pain;
My hand is on thy brow,
My spirit on thy brain;
My pity on thy heart, poor friend;
And from my fingers flow
The powers of life, and like a sign,
Seal thee from thine hour of woe;
And brood on thee, but may not blend
With thine.

'Sleep, sleep on! I love thee not;
But when I think that he
Who made and makes my lot
As full of flowers as thine of weeds,
Might have been lost like thee;
And that a hand which was not mine
Might then have charmed his agony
As I another's—my heart bleeds
For thine.

'Sleep, sleep, and with the slumber of
The dead and the unborn
Forget thy life and love;
Forget that thou must wake forever;
Forget the world's dull scorn;
Forget lost health, and the divine
Feelings which died in youth's brief morn;
And forget me, for I can never
Be thine.

'Like a cloud big with a May shower,
My soul weeps healing rain
On thee, thou withered flower!
It breathes mute music on thy sleep
Its odour calms thy brain!
Its light within thy gloomy breast
Spreads like a second youth again.
By mine thy being is to its deep
Possessed.

'The spell is done. How feel you now?'
'Better—Quite well,' replied
The sleeper.—'What would do
You good when suffering and awake?
What cure your head and side?—
'What would cure, that would kill me, Jane:
And as I must on earth abide
Awhile, yet tempt me not to break
My chain.'

The Indian Serenade

I arise from dreams of thee
In the first sweet sleep of night,
When the winds are breathing low,
And the stars are shining bright
I arise from dreams of thee,
And a spirit in my feet
Hath led me—who knows how?
To thy chamber window, Sweet!

The wandering airs they faint
On the dark, the silent stream—
The champak odours fail
Like sweet thoughts in a dream;
The nightingale's complaint,
It dies upon her heart;
As I must on thine,
Oh, beloved as thou art!

O lift me from the grass!
die! I faint! I fail!
Let thy love in kisses rain
On my lips and eyelids pale.
My cheek is cold and white, alas!
My heart beats loud and fast;—
Oh! press it to thine own again,
Where it will break at last.

Sonnet (Ye hasten to the grave!)

Ye hasten to the grave! What seek ye there,
Ye restless thoughts and busy purposes
Of the idle brain, which the world's livery wear?
O thou quick heart, which pantest to possess
All that pale Expectation feigneth fair!
Thou vainly curious mind which wouldest guess
Whence thou didst come, and whither thou must go,
And all that never yet was known would know—
Oh, whither hasten ye, that thus ye press,
With such swift feet life's green and pleasant path,
Seeking, alike from happiness and woe,
A refuge in the cavern of gray death?
O heart, and mind, and thoughts! what thing do you
Hope to inherit in the grave below?

The False Laurel and the True

'What art thou, Presumptuous, who profanest
  The wreath to mighty poets only due,
Even whilst like a forgotten moon thou wanest ?
  Touch not those leaves which for the eternal few
Who wander o'er the Paradise of fame,
  In sacred dedication ever grew:
One of the crowd thou art without a name.'
  'Ah, friend, 'tis the false laurel that I wear;
Bright though it seem, it is not the same
  As that which bound Milton's immortal hair;
Its dew is poison; and the hopes that quicken
  Under its chilling shade, though seeming fair,
Are flowers which die almost before they sicken.'

Lines to a Critic

Honey from silkworms who can gather,
Or silk from the yellow bee?
The grass may grow in winter weather
As soon as hate in me.

Hate men who cant, and men who pray,
And men who rail like thee;
An equal passion to repay
They are not coy like me.

Or seek some slave of power and gold
To be thy dear heart's mate;
Thy love will move that bigot cold
Sooner than me, thy hate.

A passion like the one I prove
Cannot divided be;
I hate thy want of truth and love—
How should I then hate thee?

On Death

They die—the dead return not—Misery
Sits near an open grave and calls them over,
A Youth with hoary hair and haggard eye—
They are the names of kindred, friend and lover,
Which he so feebly calls—they all are gone—
Fond wretch, all dead! those vacant names alone,
This most familiar scene, my pain—
These tombs—alone remain.

Misery, my sweetest friend—oh, weep no more!
Thou wilt not be consoled—I wonder not!
For I have seen thee from thy dwelling's door
Watch the calm sunset with them, and this spot
Was even as bright and calm, but transitory,
And now thy hopes are gone, thy hair is hoary;
This most familiar scene, my pain—
These tombs—alone remain.

Autumn: A Dirge

The warm sun is falling, the bleak wind is wailing,
The bare boughs are sighing, the pale flowers are dying,
And the Year
On the earth is her death-bed, in a shroud of leaves dead,
Is lying.
Come, Months, come away,
From November to May,
In your saddest array;
Follow the bier
Of the dead cold Year,
And like dim shadows watch by her sepulchre.

The chill rain is falling, the nipped worm is crawling,
The rivers are swelling, the thunder is knelling
For the Year;
The blithe swallows are flown, and the lizards each gone
To his dwelling.
Come, Months, come away;
Put on white, black and gray;
Let your light sisters play—
Ye, follow the bier
Of the dead cold Year,
And make her grave green with tear on tear.

Liberty

The fiery mountains answer each other;
Their thunderings are echoed from zone to zone;
The tempestuous oceans awake one another,
And the ice-rocks are shaken round winter's zone
When the clarion of the Typhoon is blown.

From a single cloud the lightning flashes,
Whilst a thousand isles are illumined around,
Earthquake is trampling one city to ashes,
An hundred are shuddering and tottering; the sound
Is bellowing underground.

But keener thy gaze than the lightning's glare,
And swifter thy step than the earthquake's tramp;
Thou deafenest the rage of the ocean; thy stare
Makes blind the volcanos; the sun's bright lamp
To thine is a fen-fire damp.

From billow and mountain and exhalation
The sunlight is darted through vapour and blast;
From spirit to spirit, from nation to nation,
From city to hamlet thy dawning is cast,—
And tyrants and slaves are like shadows of night
In the van of the morning light.

To the Moon

Art thou pale for weariness?
Of climbing heaven and gazing on the earth,
    Wandering companionless
Among the stars that have a different birth, –
And ever changing, like a joyless eye
That finds no object worth its constancy?

Time

Unfathomable Sea! whose waves are years,
Ocean of Time, whose waters of deep woe
Are brackish with the salt of human tears!
Thou shoreless flood, which in thy ebb and flow
Claspest the limits of mortality,
And sick of prey, yet howling on for more,
Vomitest thy wrecks on its inhospitable shore;
Treacherous in calm, and terrible in storm,
Who shall put forth on thee,
Unfathomable Sea?

A Lament

O world! O life! O time!
On whose last steps I climb,
Trembling at that where I had stood before;
When will return the glory of your prime?
No more—Oh, never more!

Out of the day and night
A joy has taken flight;
Fresh spring, and summer, and winter hoar,
Move my faint heart with grief, but with delight
No more—Oh, never more!

Far, far away, O ye

Far, far away, O ye
Halcyons of Memory,
Seek some far calmer nest
Than this abandoned breast!
No news of your false spring
To my heart's winter bring,
Once having gone, in vain
Ye come again.

Vultures, who build your bowers
High in the Future's towers,
Withered hopes on hopes are spread!
Dying joys, choked by the dead,
Will serve your beaks for prey
Many a day.

Sonnet (Lift not the painted veil)

Lift not the painted veil which those who live
Call Life: though unreal shapes be pictured there,
And it but mimic all we would believe
With colours idly spread,—behind, lurk Fear
And Hope, twin Destinies; who ever weave
Their shadows, o'er the chasm, sightless and drear.
I knew one who had lifted it—he sought,
For his lost heart was tender, things to love
But found them not, alas! nor was there aught
The world contains, the which he could approve.
Through the unheeding many he did move,
A splendour among shadows, a bright blot
Upon this gloomy scene, a Spirit that strove
For truth, and like the Preacher found it not.

The Past

Wilt thou forget the happy hours
Which we buried in Love's sweet bowers,
Heaping over their corpses cold
Blossoms and leaves, instead of mould?
Blossoms which were the joys that fell,
And leaves, the hopes that yet remain.

Forget the dead, the past? Oh, yet
There are ghosts that may take revenge for it,
Memories that make the heart a tomb,
Regrets which glide through the spirit's gloom,
And with ghastly whispers tell
That joy, once lost, is pain.

The Isle

There was a little lawny islet
By anemone and violet,
Like mosaic, paven:
And its roof was flowers and leaves
Which the summer's breath enweaves,
Where nor sun nor showers nor breeze
Pierce the pines and tallest trees,
Each a gem engraven;—
Girt by many an azure wave
With which the clouds and mountains pave
A lake's blue chasm.

The Waning Moon

And like a dying lady, lean and pale,
Who totters forth, wrapped in a gauzy veil,
Out of her chamber, led by the insane
And feeble wanderings of her fading brain,
The moon arose up in the murky east,
A white and shapeless mass.

The World's Wanderers

Tell me, thou Star, whose wings of light
Speed thee in thy fiery flight,
In what cavern of the night
  Will thy pinions close now?

Tell me, Moon, thou pale and gray
Pilgrim of heaven's homeless way,
In what depth of night or day
  Seekest thou repose now?

Weary Mind, who wanderest
Like the world's rejected guest,
Hast thou still some secret nest
  On the tree or billow?

A Bridal Song

The golden gates of Sleep unbar
Where Strength and Beauty, met together,
Kindle their image like a star
In a sea of glassy weather!
Night, with all thy stars look down,—
Darkness, weep thy holiest dew,—
Never smiled the inconstant moon
On a pair so true.
Let eyes not see their own delight;—
Haste, swift Hour, and thy flight
Oft renew.

Fairies, sprites, and angels, keep her!
Holy stars, permit no wrong!
And return to wake the sleeper,
Dawn,—ere it be long!
O joy! O fear! what will be done
In the absence of the sun!
Come along!

The Two Spirits: An Allegory

FIRST SPIRIT

O thou, who plum'd with strong desire
Wouldst float above the earth, beware!
A Shadow tracks thy flight of fire—
Night is coming!
Bright are the regions of the air,
And among the winds and beams
It were delight to wander there—
Night is coming!

SECOND SPIRIT

The deathless stars are bright above;
If I would cross the shade of night,
Within my heart is the lamp of love,
And that is day!
And the moon will smile with gentle light
On my golden plumes where'er they move;
The meteors will linger round my flight,
And make night day.

FIRST SPIRIT

But if the whirlwinds of darkness waken
Hail, and lightning, and stormy rain;
See, the bounds of the air are shaken—
Night is coming!
The red swift clouds of the hurricane
Yon declining sun have overtaken,
The clash of the hail sweeps over the plain—
Night is coming!

SECOND SPIRIT

I see the light, and I hear the sound;
I'll sail on the flood of the tempest dark,
With the calm within and the light around
Which makes night day:
And thou, when the gloom is deep and stark,
Look from thy dull earth, slumber-bound,
My moon-like flight thou then mayst mark
On high, far away.—

Some say there is a precipice
Where one vast pine is frozen to ruin
O'er piles of snow and chasms of ice
Mid Alpine mountains;
And that the languid storm pursuing
That winged shape, for ever flies
Round those hoar branches, aye renewing
Its aëry fountains.

Some say when nights are dry and dear,
And the death-dews sleep on the morass,
Sweet whispers are heard by the traveller,
Which make night day:
And a silver shape like his early love doth pass
Upborne by her wild and glittering hair,
And when he awakes on the fragrant grass,
He finds night day.

Passage of the Apennines

Listen, listen, Mary mine,
To the whisper of the Apennine,
It bursts on the roof like the thunder's roar,
Or like the sea on a northern shore,
Heard in its raging ebb and flow
By the captives pent in the cave below.
The Apennine in the light of day
Is a mighty mountain dim and gray,
Which between the earth and sky doth lay;
But when night comes, a chaos dread
On the dim starlight then is spread,
And the Apennine walks abroad with the storm,
Shrouding...

A Widow Bird Sate Mourning for Her Love

A widow bird sate mourning for her Love
Upon a wintry bough;
The frozen wind crept on above,
The freezing stream below.

There was no leaf upon the forest bare,
No flower upon the ground,
And little motion in the air
Except the mill-wheel's sound.

To — (Music, when soft voices die)

Music, when soft voices die,
Vibrates in the memory—
Odours, when sweet violets sicken,
Live within the sense they quicken.

Rose leaves, when the rose is dead,
Are heaped for the beloved's bed;
And so thy thoughts, when thou art gone,
Love itself shall slumber on.

Summer and Winter

It was a bright and cheerful afternoon,
Towards the end of the sunny month of June,
When the north wind congregates in crowds
The floating mountains of the silver clouds
From the horizon—and the stainless sky
Opens beyond them like eternity.
All things rejoiced beneath the sun; the weeds,
The river, and the cornfields, and the reeds;
The willow leaves that glanced in the light breeze,
And the firm foliage of the larger trees.

It was a winter such as when birds die
In the deep forests; and the fishes lie
Stiffened in the translucent ice, which makes
Even the mud and slime of the warm lakes
A wrinkled clod as hard as brick; and when,
Among their children, comfortable men
Gather about great fires, and yet feel cold:
Alas, then, for the homeless beggar old!

The Aziola

Do you not hear the Aziola cry?
Methinks she must be nigh,
Said Mary, as we sate
In dusk, ere stars were lit, or candles brought;
And I, who thought
This Aziola was some tedious woman,
Asked, Who is Aziola? How elate
I felt to know that it was nothing human,
No mockery of myself to fear or hate:
And Mary saw my soul,
And laughed, and said, Disquiet yourself not;
'Tis nothing but a little downy owl.

Sad Aziola! many an eventide
Thy music I had heard
By wood and stream, meadow and mountain-side,
And fields and marshes wide,—
Such as nor voice, nor lute, nor wind, nor bird,
The soul ever stirred;
Unlike and far sweeter than them all.
Sad Aziola! from that moment I
Loved thee and thy sad cry.

The Mask of Anarchy

As I lay asleep in Italy
There came a voice from over the Sea
And with great power it forth led me
To walk in the visions of Poesy.

I met Murder on the way –
He had a mask like Castlereagh –
Very smooth he looked, yet grim;
Seven blood-hounds followed him.

All were fat; and well they might
Be in admirable plight,
For one by one, and two by two,
He tossed the human hearts to chew
Which from his wide cloak he drew.

Next came Fraud, and he had on,
Like Eldon, an ermined gown;
His big tears, for he wept well,
Turned to mill-stones as they fell:

And the little children, who
Round his feet played to and fro,
Thinking every tear a gem,
Had their brains knocked out by them.

Clothed with the Bible, as with light,
And the shadows of the night,
Like Sidmouth, next, Hypocrisy
On a crocodile rode by.

And many more Destructions played
In this ghastly masquerade,
All disguised, even to the eyes,
Like Bishops, lawyers, peers, or spies.

Last came Anarchy: he rode
On a white horse, splashed with blood;
He was pale even to the lips,
Like Death in the Apocalypse.

And he wore a kingly crown;
And in his grasp a sceptre shone;
On his brow this mark I saw—
'I AM GOD, AND KING, AND LAW!'

With a pace stately and fast,
Over English land he passed,
Trampling to a mire of blood
The adoring multitude.

And a mighty troop around,
With their trampling shook the ground,
Waving each a bloody sword,
For the service of their Lord.

And with glorious triumph, they
Rode through England proud and gay,
Drunk as with intoxication
Of the wine of desolation.

O'er fields and towns, from sea to sea,
Passed the Pageant swift and free,

Tearing up, and trampling down;
Till they came to London town.

And each dweller, panic-stricken,
Felt his heart with terror sicken
Hearing the tempestuous cry
Of the triumph of Anarchy.

For with pomp to meet him came,
Clothed in arms like blood and flame,
The hired murderers, who did sing
'Thou art God, and Law, and King.

'We have waited, weak and lone
For thy coming, Mighty One!
Our Purses are empty, our swords are cold,
Give us glory, and blood, and gold.'

Lawyers and priests, a motley crowd,
To the earth their pale brows bowed;
Like a bad prayer not over loud,
Whispering—'Thou art Law and God.'—

Then all cried with one accord,
'Thou art King, and God and Lord;
Anarchy, to thee we bow,
Be thy name made holy now!'

And Anarchy, the skeleton,
Bowed and grinned to every one,
As well as if his education
Had cost ten millions to the nation.

For he knew the Palaces
Of our Kings were rightly his;
His the sceptre, crown and globe,
And the gold-inwoven robe.

So he sent his slaves before
To seize upon the Bank and Tower,
And was proceeding with intent
To meet his pensioned Parliament

When one fled past, a maniac maid,
And her name was Hope, she said:
But she looked more like Despair,
And she cried out in the air:

'My father Time is weak and gray
With waiting for a better day;
See how idiot-like he stands,
Fumbling with his palsied hands!

He has had child after child,
And the dust of death is piled
Over every one but me—
Misery, oh, Misery!'

Then she lay down in the street,
Right before the horses' feet,
Expecting, with a patient eye,
Murder, Fraud, and Anarchy.

When between her and her foes
A mist, a light, an image rose,

Small at first, and weak, and frail
Like the vapour of a vale:

Till as clouds grow on the blast,
Like tower-crowned giants striding fast,
And glare with lightnings as they fly,
And speak in thunder to the sky,

It grew—a Shape arrayed in mail
Brighter than the viper's scale,
And upborne on wings whose grain
Was as the light of sunny rain.

On its helm, seen far away,
A planet, like the Morning's, lay;
And those plumes its light rained through
Like a shower of crimson dew.

With step as soft as wind it passed
O'er the heads of men—so fast
That they knew the presence there,
And looked,—but all was empty air.

As flowers beneath May's footstep waken,
As stars from Night's loose hair are shaken,
As waves arise when loud winds call,
Thoughts sprung where'er that step did fall.

And the prostrate multitude
Looked—and ankle-deep in blood,
Hope, that maiden most serene,
Was walking with a quiet mien:

And Anarchy, the ghastly birth,
Lay dead earth upon the earth;
The Horse of Death tameless as wind
Fled, and with his hoofs did grind
To dust the murderers thronged behind.

A rushing light of clouds and splendour,
A sense awakening and yet tender
Was heard and felt—and at its close
These words of joy and fear arose

As if their own indignant Earth
Which gave the sons of England birth
Had felt their blood upon her brow,
And shuddering with a mother's throe

Had turned every drop of blood
By which her face had been bedewed
To an accent unwithstood,—
As if her heart had cried aloud:

'Men of England, heirs of Glory,
Heroes of unwritten story,
Nurslings of one mighty Mother,
Hopes of her, and one another;

'Rise like Lions after slumber
In unvanquishable number,
Shake your chains to earth like dew
Which in sleep had fallen on you—
Ye are many—they are few.

'What is Freedom?—ye can tell
That which slavery is, too well—
For its very name has grown
To an echo of your own.

'Tis to work and have such pay
As just keeps life from day to day
In your limbs, as in a cell
For the tyrants' use to dwell,

'So that ye for them are made
Loom, and plough, and sword, and spade,
With or without your own will bent
To their defence and nourishment.

'Tis to see your children weak
With their mothers pine and peak,
When the winter winds are bleak,—
They are dying whilst I speak.

'Tis to hunger for such diet
As the rich man in his riot
Casts to the fat dogs that lie
Surfeiting beneath his eye;

'Tis to let the Ghost of Gold
Take from Toil a thousandfold
More that e'er its substance could
In the tyrannies of old.

'Paper coin—that forgery
Of the title-deeds, which ye

Hold to something of the worth
Of the inheritance of Earth.

'Tis to be a slave in soul
And to hold no strong control
Over your own wills, but be
All that others make of ye.

'And at length when ye complain
With a murmur weak and vain
'Tis to see the Tyrant's crew
Ride over your wives and you—
Blood is on the grass like dew.

'Then it is to feel revenge
Fiercely thirsting to exchange
Blood for blood—and wrong for wrong—
Do not thus when ye are strong.

'Birds find rest, in narrow nest
When weary of their wingèd quest
Beasts find fare, in woody lair
When storm and snow are in the air.

'Asses, swine, have litter spread
And with fitting food are fed;
All things have a home but one—
Thou, Oh, Englishman, hast none!

'This is slavery—savage men
Or wild beasts within a den

Would endure not as ye do—
But such ills they never knew.

'What art thou Freedom? O! could slaves
Answer from their living graves
This demand—tyrants would flee
Like a dream's dim imagery:

'Thou art not, as impostors say,
A shadow soon to pass away,
A superstition, and a name
Echoing from the cave of Fame.

'For the labourer thou art bread,
And a comely table spread
From his daily labour come
In a neat and happy home.

'Thou art clothes, and fire, and food
For the trampled multitude—
No—in countries that are free
Such starvation cannot be
As in England now we see.

'To the rich thou art a check,
When his foot is on the neck
Of his victim, thou dost make
That he treads upon a snake.

'Thou art Justice—ne'er for gold
May thy righteous laws be sold

As laws are in England—thou
Shield'st alike the high and low.

'Thou art Wisdom—Freemen never
Dream that God will damn for ever
All who think those things untrue
Of which Priests make such ado.

'Thou art Peace—never by thee
Would blood and treasure wasted be
As tyrants wasted them, when all
Leagued to quench thy flame in Gaul.

'What if English toil and blood
Was poured forth, even as a flood?
It availed, Oh, Liberty,
To dim, but not extinguish thee.

'Thou art Love—the rich have kissed
Thy feet, and like him following Christ,
Give their substance to the free
And through the rough world follow thee,

'Or turn their wealth to arms, and make
War for thy belovèd sake
On wealth, and war, and fraud—whence they
Drew the power which is their prey.

'Science, Poetry, and Thought
Are thy lamps; they make the lot
Of the dwellers in a cot
So serene, they curse it not.

'Spirit, Patience, Gentleness,
All that can adorn and bless
Art thou—let deeds, not words, express
Thine exceeding loveliness.

'Let a great Assembly be
Of the fearless and the free
On some spot of English ground
Where the plains stretch wide around.

'Let the blue sky overhead,
The green earth on which ye tread,
All that must eternal be
Witness the solemnity.

'From the corners uttermost
Of the bounds of English coast;
From every hut, village, and town
Where those who live and suffer moan,

'From the workhouse and the prison
Where pale as corpses newly risen,
Women, children, young and old
Groan for pain, and weep for cold—

'From the haunts of daily life
Where is waged the daily strife
With common wants and common cares
Which sows the human heart with tares—

'Lastly from the palaces
Where the murmur of distress

Echoes, like the distant sound
Of a wind alive around

'Those prison halls of wealth and fashion,
Where some few feel such compassion
For those who groan, and toil, and wail
As must make their brethren pale—

'Ye who suffer woes untold,
Or to feel, or to behold
Your lost country bought and sold
With a price of blood and gold—

'Let a vast assembly be,
And with great solemnity
Declare with measured words that ye
Are, as God has made ye, free—

'Be your strong and simple words
Keen to wound as sharpened swords,
And wide as targets let them be,
With their shade to cover ye.

'Let the tyrants pour around
With a quick and startling sound,
Like the loosening of a sea,
Troops of armed emblazonry.

Let the charged artillery drive
Till the dead air seems alive
With the clash of clanging wheels,
And the tramp of horses' heels.

'Let the fixèd bayonet
Gleam with sharp desire to wet
Its bright point in English blood
Looking keen as one for food.

'Let the horsemen's scimitars
Wheel and flash, like sphereless stars
Thirsting to eclipse their burning
In a sea of death and mourning.

'Stand ye calm and resolute,
Like a forest close and mute,
With folded arms and looks which are
Weapons of unvanquished war,

'And let Panic, who outspeeds
The career of armèd steeds
Pass, a disregarded shade
Through your phalanx undismayed.

'Let the laws of your own land,
Good or ill, between ye stand
Hand to hand, and foot to foot,
Arbiters of the dispute,

'The old laws of England—they
Whose reverend heads with age are gray,
Children of a wiser day;
And whose solemn voice must be
Thine own echo—Liberty!

'On those who first should violate
Such sacred heralds in their state
Rest the blood that must ensue,
And it will not rest on you.

'And if then the tyrants dare
Let them ride among you there,
Slash, and stab, and maim, and hew,—
What they like, that let them do.

'With folded arms and steady eyes,
And little fear, and less surprise,
Look upon them as they slay
Till their rage has died away.

'Then they will return with shame
To the place from which they came,
And the blood thus shed will speak
In hot blushes on their cheek.

'Every woman in the land
Will point at them as they stand—
They will hardly dare to greet
Their acquaintance in the street.

'And the bold, true warriors
Who have hugged Danger in wars
Will turn to those who would be free,
Ashamed of such base company.

'And that slaughter to the Nation
Shall steam up like inspiration,

Eloquent, oracular;
A volcano heard afar.

'And these words shall then become
Like Oppression's thundered doom
Ringing through each heart and brain,
Heard again—again—again—

'Rise like Lions after slumber
In unvanquishable number—
Shake your chains to earth like dew
Which in sleep had fallen on you—
Ye are many—they are few.'

An Ariette for Music

As the moon's soft splendour
O'er the faint cold starlight of Heaven
Is thrown,
So your voice most tender
To the strings without soul had then given
Its own.

The stars will awaken,
Though the moon sleep a full hour later,
To-night;
No leaf will be shaken
Whilst the dews of your melody scatter
Delight.

Though the sound overpowers,
Sing again, with your dear voice revealing
A tone
Of some world far from ours,
Where music and moonlight and feeling
Are one.

England in 1819

An old, mad, blind, despised, and dying king,—
Princes, the dregs of their dull race, who flow
Through public scorn, mud from a muddy spring,—
Rulers who neither see, nor feel, nor know,
But leech-like to their fainting country cling,
Till they drop, blind in blood, without a blow,—
A people starved and stabbed in the untilled field,—
An army which liberticide and prey
Makes as a two-edged sword to all who wield,—
Golden and sanguine laws which tempt and slay;
Religion Christless, Godless, a book sealed,—
A Senate—Time's worst statute unrepealed,—
Are graves from which a glorious Phantom may
Burst to illumine our tempestuous day.

Remembrance

Swifter far than summer's flight—
Swifter far than youth's delight—
Swifter far than happy night,
Art thou come and gone—
As the earth when leaves are dead,
As the night when sleep is sped,
As the heart when joy is fled,
I am left lone, alone.

The swallow summer comes again—
The owlet night resumes her reign—
But the wild-swan youth is fain
To fly with thee, false as thou.—
My heart each day desires the morrow;
Sleep itself is turned to sorrow;
Vainly would my winter borrow
Sunny leaves from any bough.

Lilies for a bridal bed—
Roses for a matron's head—
Violets for a maiden dead—
Pansies let MY flowers be:
On the living grave I bear
Scatter them without a tear—
Let no friend, however dear,
Waste one hope, one fear for me.

A Roman's Chamber

In the cave which wild weeds cover
Wait for thine aethereal lover;
For the pallid moon is waning,
O'er the spiral cypress hanging
And the moon no cloud is staining.

It was once a Roman's chamber,
Where he kept his darkest revels.
And the wild weeds twine and clamber;
It was then a chasm for devils.

To Mary Shelley

The world is dreary,
And I am weary
Of wandering on without thee, Mary;
A joy was erewhile
In thy voice and thy smile,
And 'tis gone, when I should be gone too, Mary.

To Sophia (Miss Stacey)

Thou art fair, and few are fairer
Of the Nymphs of earth or ocean;
They are robes that fit the wearer—
Those soft limbs of thine, whose motion
Ever falls and shifts and glances
As the life within them dances.

Thy deep eyes, a double Planet,
Gaze the wisest into madness
With soft clear fire,—the winds that fan it
Are those thoughts of tender gladness
Which, like zephyrs on the billow,
Make thy gentle soul their pillow.

If, whatever face thou paintest
In those eyes, grows pale with pleasure,
If the fainting soul is faintest
When it hears thy harp's wild measure,
Wonder not that when thou speakest
Of the weak my heart is weakest.

As dew beneath the wind of morning,
As the sea which whirlwinds waken,
As the birds at thunder's warning,
As aught mute yet deeply shaken,
As one who feels an unseen spirit
Is my heart when thine is near it.

To — (I fear thy kisses)

I fear thy kisses, gentle maiden,
Thou needest not fear mine;
My spirit is too deeply laden
Ever to burthen thine.

I fear thy mien, thy tones, thy motion,
Thou needest not fear mine;
Innocent is the heart's devotion
With which I worship thine.

The Poet's Dream

On a poet's lips I slept
Dreaming like a love adept
In the sound his breathing kept;
Nor seeks nor finds he mortal blisses,
But feeds on the aerial kisses,
Of shapes that haunt thoughts wildernesses.
He will watch from dawn to gloom
The lake reflected sun illume
The yellow bees in the ivy-bloom
Nor heed nor see, what things they be;
But from these create he can
Forms more real than living man,
Nurslings of immortality!
One of these awakened me,
And I sped to succour thee.

Index of First Lines